Conflicted

Voices of Central American Migrants

by Catalina Rodríguez Tapia

CONFLICTED

VOICES OF CENTRAL
AMERICAN MIGRANTS

CATALINA RODRÍGUEZ TAPIA

NEW DEGREE PRESS

CONFLICTED

Voices of Central American Migrants

ISBN   978-1-63676-524-2   *Paperback*

        978-1-63676-061-2   *Kindle Ebook*

        978-1-63676-062-9   *Ebook*

To all those Central Americans living far away from home.

CONTENTS

———

INTRODUCTION   11

PART I.   **HOW DID WE GET HERE?**   **19**
CHAPTER 1.   THE UNFINISHED CENTRAL AMERICAN
              PEACE ACCORDS   21
CHAPTER 2.   FAMILY FIRST   33
CHAPTER 3.   THE FACE OF INJUSTICE   41
CHAPTER 4.   THE ABANDONED YOUTH   51

PART II.   **WHAT IS GOING ON IN CENTRAL AMERICA?**   **67**
CHAPTER 5.   WHEN THE RISK IS WORTH THE JOURNEY   69
CHAPTER 6.   THE ALLURE OF LEAVING   81
CHAPTER 7.   SUB-STATES   91
CHAPTER 8.   THE DEATH OF ENTREPRENEURSHIP   101
CHAPTER 9.   WHAT RESILIENCE REALLY LOOKS LIKE   109

PART III.   **WHERE DO WE GO FROM HERE?**   **127**
CHAPTER 10.   #DÓNDE-ESTÁ-EL-DINERO   129
CHAPTER 11.   LOCATION, LOCATION, LOCATION   143
CHAPTER 12.   A PORTAL TO CENTRAL AMERICA   151
CHAPTER 13.   YOU CAN'T JUDGE A COWBOY BY HIS HAT   161
CONCLUSION: ILLUSION OF PROGRESS?   173
ACKNOWLEDGEMENT   181
APPENDIX   185

La América Olvidada

Entre el Pacífico y Atlántico
Se encuentra un Istmo descartado
Hundido por años de negligencia continental
Y distinguido por un son, bien distinto a los demás

En esa América olvidada-
Tierra de los Mayas
Ex concubina de España
Juguete del Norte
Se respiró libertad en 1821- y hoy en día se respira dictadura
O resentimiento entre sus maras

La mano dura que machuca y no resuelve
Opresión, la que opaca la voz de la gente
Donde la falta de opciones se resuelve más allá del Río Grande
Y tras el Río Grande se respira muerte

Pero en la América olvidada
A veces se respira felicidad-
dos aguas cristalinas que se enlazan en Panamá
los tambores garífunas en las Islas de la Bahía
que se oyen hasta la ruinas de Copán

Mientras el tico, hablando del ambiente y de la paz
se arrima a Nicaragua, y se encuentra fiesta y bacanal
Y los chapines se revuelcan entre volcanes y ruinas
Con un salvadoreño cuyos sueños no terminan.

INTRODUCTION

I fanned myself with the stack of questionnaires in my hand and reluctantly made my way toward a stranger. It was a hot summer day in 2015. I was an undergraduate student at Georgetown University in Washington, DC, and a long way from home.

I had never been to Columbia Heights before, but it quickly felt like home—vendors selling plantain chips (*tajaditas*, as I would call them), the distinct smell of cheese oozing out of a pupusa that sizzled on a hot skillet in the sidewalk, and the incessant Spanish chatter in accents I quickly recognized were from different Central American countries. In fact, this neighborhood was historically Central American and particularly Salvadoran, since government employees and international agency personnel began sponsoring Central American domestic workers and childcare providers in the 1970s, forming a primarily Salvadoran enclave in Columbia Heights.[1]

---

1   Ana Patricia Rodríguez, "Becoming 'Wachintonians' Salvadorans in the Washington, D.C., Metropolitan Area," *Washington History* (Fall 2016: 5)

That enclave was the reason I'd been assigned to this neighborhood and not elsewhere in metropolitan DC. As an intern at the Inter-American Dialogue, a think tank that analyzes Western Hemisphere affairs, my task was to collect data on migration flows, remittance patterns, and political views. This task required me to select strangers at random, ask them invasive questions about their personal lives, and hope they would answer.

Where are you from? Do you send money back home? How much? I'd read the questions to my interviewees and write their responses on the questionnaire. The nature of the questions grew increasingly sensitive. *Why did you migrate to the United States?* And the most invasive question of all, *Are you undocumented?* Invading the privacy of my fellow Central Americans made me uneasy. But few of these strangers seemed to consider the questions of a twenty-year-old as invasive at all. Rather, many individuals welcomed the opportunity to tell their story—to be heard.

My name is Catalina Rodríguez Tapia. My interest in Central American affairs has been fueled by my experiences and exposure to a region that has always been home to my family. I am a Central American migrant, have family who are Central American migrants, and have parents who are Central American migrants. I was raised in Honduras and lived there for eighteen years, but I am Costa Rican. Now I live in the United States and am not American. When a 1979 revolution brought about unrest in Nicaragua, part of my family was expelled to Costa Rica. Civil war in El Salvador forced one of my mother's best friends to flee with her family in 1980, requiring them to immigrate to Maryland to start a new life.

The stories I explore in this book are not unlike those of my family and friends. Nor are they unlike what I encountered that day in Columbia Heights. That day, I met people from a myriad of backgrounds: naturalized citizens, undocumented migrants, students like myself, workers, people who were thriving, people who were struggling, Salvadorans, Hondurans, Nicaraguans, Guatemalans, and mixes.

Despite these differences among all of them, there was a similarity. They had all left their home of origin in Central America.

The key question is *why?*

The story of one of the Salvadoran migrants I interviewed left a deep impression. When we met, he was in his late 60s. Back home in El Salvador, he had been a middle-class family man, earning his living as a local store manager. He seemed to have everything going for him at that point, he told me. But then one day, a letter arrived at his place of business, and he knew his life would be forever changed.

In El Salvador, gangs often build their organizations' wealth by committing a form of extortion. They call it the *impuesto de guerra*, which translates to "war tax." Gang members impose these fees on businesses, requiring payment in order to "avoid casualties." The man—we'll call him Roberto—lived and worked in a gang-dominated area. When he received a letter, demanding payment of the impuesto de guerra, Roberto knew the risks it implied. So, he paid it exactly as instructed every month—always the same amount and always on the due date—just as he paid his other bills. This, he hoped, would keep his family safe.

Before long, the gang increased the impuesto de guerra, and Roberto found a way to raise the funds. But the gang repeatedly increased the fee until, eventually, paying the impuesto de guerra threatened to bankrupt his business. Without other options and without a single doubt in his mind, he packed up and with his family left El Salvador forever.

When I interviewed Roberto on the streets in Columbia Heights, years had passed, and his resolve remained unchanged.

"Did I want to leave?" he asked rhetorically, "Of course not. That's where I grew up. That was my home. That was my city. But the circumstances were such that it was inevitable. The local police were controlled by the gang members, so I couldn't rely on them. The state had little power in territories governed by the gang members, so I couldn't denounce them to state authorities either. And the prospects of finding another job to pay off the war tax were zero. I did not want to leave. I had to."

Today Roberto is one of the nearly 1.4 million immigrants from El Salvador living in the United States, representing one fifth of El Salvador's population. Similarly, Hondurans in the US comprise approximately 7 percent of its population, and 5 percent of Guatemala's.[2] [3]

Roberto's story, like so many others I heard in Columbia Heights that day, echoed the stories I'd grown up with in Honduras. I'd heard the stories of desperate friends or neighbors—their family members having been kidnapped or even killed—forced to flee the country for their safety. I'd heard the stories of people who wished to find opportunities elsewhere. And I had my own story: the heartfelt acknowledgement on the day I left Honduras that—despite my love for the country—I would likely never live there again. We all shared a belief that in another country, although the grass was not completely green, it was greener than at home.

Out-migration has daunted the governments of El Salvador, Guatemala, and Honduras for many reasons. For one, out-migration has led to an unfortunate brain drain of the region's human capital. A study by the World Bank suggests that the loss in human capital associated with a ten-year outflow of adults since 1990—as measured by foregone local wages—represents 1.9 percent of the gross domestic product (GDP) in El Salvador, 1.5 percent in Honduras, and 1.0 percent in Guatemala.[4]

2   Steven A. Camarota and Karen Zeigler, "Central American Immigrant Population Increased Nearly 28-Fold since 1970," *Center for Immigration Studies,* (Washington DC, November 2018).

3   "Population 2019," World Bank Data.

4   Giselle del Carmen and Liliana D. Sousa, "Human Capital Outflows: Selection into Migration from the Northern Triangle," World Bank, (Policy Research Working Paper 883, 2018).

Furthermore, the 2014 unaccompanied child crisis brought greater attention to the humanitarian crisis unfolding on the United States-Mexico border.

According to Border Patrol, apprehensions of unaccompanied children rose from 38,833 in the fiscal year of 2013 to 47,017 in only the first eight months of fiscal year 2014.[5] That's a 20 percent increase, without counting the remaining four months of the year.

As a response to the crisis, the governments of the area often referred to as the Northern Triangle—which includes El Salvador, Guatemala, and Honduras—were supported by the US through the Plan of the Alliance for Prosperity. For these purposes, just in fiscal year 2016, US Congress allocated $750 million dollars in support of the program with the ultimate goal of curbing out-migration.[6] Under this framework, the governments also received technical support in drafting a plan with the Inter-American Development Bank (IADB) through a five-year plan seeking to stimulate the productive sector, develop human capital, improve public safety, and strengthen institutions.[7]

The United States' urgency to focus on these countries makes sense because it is the main destination country, making it a strategic decision in the face of the child crisis. In 2018, an

---

5   Diana Villiers Negroponte, "The Surge in Unaccompanied Children from Central America: A Humanitarian Crisis at Our Border," Brookings Institution, (July 2014).

6   "¿Qué ofrece el Plan Alianza para la Prosperidad?" Inter-American Dialogue: 1-2.

7   "Plan of the Alliance for Prosperity in the Northern Triangle: A Road Map," Inter-American Development Bank, (September 2014: 1-10).

overwhelming 91 percent of all Northern Triangle emigrants chose the United States as their destination country.[8]

Additionally, the tactics to finance areas such as the productive sector, human capital, public safety, and stronger institutions seems to make sense. The data has always pointed toward issues of economic opportunities and crime as key factors that lead to out-migration. Analyses conducted by the Inter-American Dialogue show that in Honduras, a 1 percent increase in homicides drives migration by 120 percent, in Guatemala by 100 percent, and in El Salvador by 188 percent. Economic informality, or economic activity that operates outside the legal and regulatory frameworks, also affects out-migration. Economic informality can be as simple as a food stand that is not formally registered and thus operates while evading taxes and are subsequently also excluded from social security. A 1 percent increase in the size of economic informality drives migration by 12 percent in Honduras, 4 percent in Guatemala, and 27 percent in El Salvador.[9]

However, beyond what the data may show, the migrants I spoke to made it clear that their reasons for leaving were more complicated than just lack of opportunities or violence.

In Roberto's case, there was a clear conflict going on his mind, and a myriad of factors that pushed him to leave. He faced insecurity; his business had been crushed, and the

---

8   Manuel Orozco, "Central American Migration: Current Changes and Development Implications." Inter-American Dialogue (November 2018: 8).

9   Manuel Orozco, "Central American Migration: Current Changes and Development Implications."

police—the state entity responsible for protecting him in the face of this injustice—had failed to help him. In fact, it wasn't one factor or another; it was a mix of many factors rooted in the weakness of the state, affecting the provision of basic services and protection, that pushed him away.

For a long time, analysts and policymakers have blamed factors like violence or lack of economic opportunities for out-migration, without realizing these are just symptoms of a deeper problem: historically weak states. By shedding light on some of the real struggles some people face at home, my hope is that policymakers, analysts, and people who care, will refocus the attention to unraveling some of the intricacies of these weak Central American states.

Through this book, I explore the mindset of conflicted migrants—migrants whose states have failed them, whose states are broken after unresolved social issues dating back to the region's civil wars and social revolutions in the 1970s. Their states have not provided citizens with proper security, quality education, and basic needs. They have not supported people in urgent need of a job. These failures laid the groundwork for people to decide to leave their countries. By sharing these stories, I hope to reach a larger audience so more people can empathize with the complexities of why Central Americans continue to leave their countries.

PART I

HOW DID WE
GET HERE?

CHAPTER 1

THE UNFINISHED CENTRAL AMERICAN PEACE ACCORDS

———

One night, Guillermo was driving his taxi in the streets of San Miguel, his hometown in El Salvador. He was a university student but was unable to attend school because of grim events that had unfolded a couple of days prior. An attack that had paralyzed the entire country. Instead of staying at home, Guillermo decided he would work to earn some income; after all, he had a pregnant wife and a boy to take care of. What happened that night, paired with the incidents leading up to that day, pushed Guillermo to the limit. It made him decide it was time to leave.

The year was 1989, and El Salvador had just experienced a historical event: The Last Offensive, or "La última ofensiva." The country was in ruins. Ninety-five percent of bridges had been destroyed. People sometimes had no electricity for weeks at a time.

The chaos was rooted in the rivalry between guerrilla fighters and the country's military. Guerrillas were freedom-fighters, people who believed that the government was unfair and demanded more rights for the country's citizens. Guillermo confessed the reason he wasn't interested in the movement. The guerrilla fighters originally had good intentions. They were the ones who fought with the government when they increased prices. They were the ones who protested. They represented human rights.

However, the moment they refocused their attention on gaining political power, the guerrillas' movement lost meaning to him. They resorted to violence and recruited people to join their fight, sometimes forcefully. Guillermo remembers how they would sweep through neighborhoods, telling people that they could either join the fight or leave their homes. On the other hand, the government had no issues opening fire on civilians. Guillermo, neither a guerrilla fighter nor a supporter of the military, was stuck in the middle.

On a November afternoon, Guillermo tuned into a radio program called Radio Venceremos and heard the newscaster issue an alarming warning: for civilians to keep away from gas stations, hospitals, and other public locations where the military had been gathering in recent days. The warning foreshadowed the big event. There would be an attack—a big one.

"La última ofensiva" began on a Friday night, during the San Miguel Carnaval. Heavily armed guerrilla fighters opened fire in several public areas as the festivities were taking place. They carried extra rifles to pass to citizens willing to join the cause. The street was a war zone, where everyone from guerrilla fighters, to military officers, and even innocent civilians were at risk.

The government's response to the attack was to summon the air force. Using planes and helicopters, they opened fire in the residential areas, killing guerrilla fighters and civilians alike. Guillermo was lucky to not be in the residential areas that were targeted that day, but he distinctly remembers the helicopter that soared through the sky and continued aiming and attacking, hit after hit. The guerrilla fighters retaliated, and managed to hit one of the helicopters, which began soaring out of control. When the helicopter fell, it exploded. Guillermo said it looked like a mushroom, almost like a mini nuclear bomb. Meanwhile, other air force troops continued killing anyone who crossed their path.

Bodies were scattered throughout the streets after these attacks, too many to hold a funeral for. "The people in affected neighborhoods burned the bodies, and at night you could smell the burning flesh, burning hair, and burning bones."

For a while after the incident, Guillermo's father, who lived in the United States, insisted he join him. Despite what was going on, Guillermo was hesitant.

Until one night when he was driving in his taxi, looking for passengers to generate income in the middle of a war.

Guillermo was riding through the Central Market when a man stopped him, got in the back seat, and said nothing. This rattled him; most of the passengers would immediately say where they were going and ask how much it would cost.

"Where should I take you?" Guillermo asked.

"Take me to Milagro de la Paz, and if I don't find what I am looking for, I am going to need you to take me somewhere else," said the man.

At this point, Guillermo was not only nervous because of the man's strange demeanor and dry tone. The address terrified him. Milagro de la Paz was a dangerous part of town

As is customary, Guillermo politely requested an exact address.

"Let me look for the paper." The man rifled through his bag, then pulled out something and placed it in the front surface of the car, right in Guillermo's view. It was a grenade. And then he pulled out a second grenade.

"That's when I froze," Guillermo told me.

The passenger, who Guillermo quickly learned was an off-duty military officer, then pulled out a gun. Guillermo couldn't help but think this was the end, with two grenades staring him in the face.

"I am looking for someone who used my gun to kill some-one else," he explained to Guillermo. "If we don't find him at this address, then we will have to search for him in this other address."

The military officer, an authority figure, was using Guill-ermo to seek revenge, asking him to become an accomplice in murder.

"Back then, I would have charged one hundred colones for the ride. I told him that I couldn't continue. I was terrified that this guy would not take it lightly, but he simply said that I wouldn't get paid. Honestly, I didn't care if I didn't get one hundred colones."

The military officer let him go. However, after that incident, Guillermo took his father up on his offer and planned to move to the United States. He was in a middle of a war that was not his to fight, and he had had enough. He sold the taxi to get some cash and decided to embark on the dangerous journey up north with his family.

The civil wars, violence and repression are not unique to El Salvador.

With the exception of Costa Rica, the Central American region went through a series of political regimes before consolidating into democracies, as illustrated below.[10] Although these countries were going through different regime changes, they were all characterized by dominant military involvement.

---

10 John A. Booth, Christine J. Wade, and Thomas W. Walker, *Understanding Central America: Costa Rica, Nicaragua, El Salvador, Guatemala and Honduras: from Independence to the Present* (Boulder, CO: Westview, 2005), 27.

Central American Regime Types (1970-2004)				
Costa Rica	**El Salvador**	**Guatemala**	**Honduras**	**Nicaragua**
Civilian Democratic	Military authoritarianism	Military Authoritarianism	Military Authoritarianism	Personalistic Military
	Reformist Military (1979)	Reformist Military (1982)	Reformist Military (1980)	Revolutionary (1979)
	Civilian Transitional (1984)	Civilian Transitional (1985)	Civilian Transitional (1982)	Revolutionary transitional (1984)
	Civilian democratic (1992)	Civilian democratic (1996)	Civilian democratic (1996)	Civilian democratic (1987)

Source: Booth, Wade and Walker (2005), Understanding Central America, 27

El Salvador, Guatemala and Honduras, followed very similar trajectories; they began as military authoritarian regimes dominated by a military establishment and became reformist military regimes in the 1980s, with militaries willing to democratize. In the mid-1980s, they transitioned to civilian transitional regimes, in which elected civilian rulers were backed by a strong military. All of these steps transpired before becoming democracies. Costa Rica, on the other hand, disbanded its military in 1948, and established a democracy early on.

This transition from military authoritarian regimes to democracies was a painful transition characterized by civil wars, as Guillermo experienced in the flesh. His story is just a snippet of years of war and violence.

El Salvador, in particular, was characterized by a history of social unrest since the 16th century. As certain groups and families took over plots of land, inequality increased. Even though 95 percent of the population were indigenous people or mestizos (mixed race, often of Spanish and indigenous descent), they were deprived of the landowning elite's resources and riches. The landholders, a group of powerful families, ruled the country through a long series of military dictatorships.

However, as is the case in states with great inequality and dictatorships, those at the lower socioeconomic tier were unhappy. In 1932, Agustín Farabundo Martí led a peasant revolution against those fourteen powerful families who had held power for so long. It was a call against the unjust structures of power in which only a select few held the majority of resources. The state response was a massive military reprisal called *la matanza* (the slaughter). Approximately thirty thousand civilians, most of whom were indigenous people who worked in the land, were killed by the military.[11]

In March of 1980, Archbishop Oscar Romero became one of the central voices against the dictatorship's human rights violations. However, he was too vocal for the incumbent dictatorship. During one of his masses, he spoke about the military's obligation to cease their assassination of civilians—of innocent people. Just as he was officiating the Mass, he was assassinated by a sniper.[12]

The tragedy did not end there. When 250,000 mourners gathered in the Archbishop's funeral, snipers attacked the crowd. Forty-two people were killed and two hundred were wounded. As a BBC reporter in that time reported, "Tens of thousands of mourners who had gathered for Romero's funeral mass in front of the cathedral in San Salvador were filmed fleeing in terror as army gunners on the rooftops around the square opened fire…One person who was there told us he remembered the piles of shoes left behind by those

---

11 "El Salvador" The Center for Justice & Accountability.

12 "El Salvador."

who escaped with their lives."[13] That day officially began the civil war in El Salvador.

Around the same time, the Farabundo Martí National Liberation Front (FMLN), a guerrilla movement that later became a political party, developed as an expression in support of Martí and what he represented when he was alive. This party is still one of the popular parties in power but has done little to address the issues they fought for years before.

A consequence of the war was out-migration: people like Guillermo fleeing the conditions at home. From 1970 to 1980, as the war raged, the population of El Salvadorans in the United States blew up from sixteen thousand to ninety-four thousand, a 488 percent increase. From 1980 to 1990, the amount increased once again to 465,000 people, a 389 percent increase.[14]

I learned how strong the Salvadoran presence was in the United States when I moved to Washington, DC, seven years ago. I already knew Salvadorans before I came; my mother's close friend was from El Salvador and had moved there with her family in the 1990s because of the civil war. In the first couple of months after I arrived in the capital, I met Salvadorans left and right, many of whom quickly admitted that they had come because of the civil war.

---

13 "Salvador Archbishop Assassinated By Sniper While Officiating at Mass; Churchman Was Known as Outspoken Advocate of Justice and Rights Advocate of Human Rights Archbishop Romero Slain in El Salvador," *New York Times* (March 1980).

14 Cecilia Menjívar and Andrea Gómez Cervantes, "El Salvador: Civil War, Natural Disasters, and Gang Violence Drive Migration," *Migration Policy Institute*, (August 29, 2018)

Back then, I was a freshman in Georgetown University. As a student, I got most of my meals from the university's cafeteria, a large brick structure framed with an overarching sign that spells "O'Donovan" on the front of the building's façade. Nobody called it that, however. Everyone called it Leo's.

To access Leo's, we needed to swipe our student cards, also known as GoCards. Every time we walked in, the cafeteria staff would greet us at the entrance to swipe our card and allow entry. They were basically like bouncers for the cafeteria. This is how I met my favorite cafeteria "bouncer," Pedro.

Pedro was from El Salvador. He was in his 60s and had a jovial spirit. He always offered a smile to the students as they walked into the cafeteria.

At first, I had no idea he was a fellow Central American. I saw his name tag and assumed he was a Spanish-speaker. One day, I decided I would greet him in Spanish.

"Hola. ¿Cómo está?"

He smiled and responded. "Hola muchacha, muy bien. ¿Y usted?"

From then on, he always spoke to me in Spanish when I walked into the cafeteria.

One day, I decided to pick up food from the Grab n' Go so I could eat it at the library. It was midterm season, so I was very stressed out.

Pedro greeted me at the entrance. I explained that I wouldn't be going into the cafeteria. I picked out my selection of foods: a sandwich, a yogurt, and a juice box. As I told Pedro that that would be it, he looked at me and said "Muchacha, take some more! At least a cookie, I promise I won't tell! It's the least I can do for a stressed-out student." I smiled and took him up on the offer. I remember how this made me smile and this quickly sparked a conversation.

Pedro asked me where I was from. I told him from Costa Rica, but raised in Honduras, and he got excited "We are neighbors! I am from El Salvador, but I have been living here for the past twenty-five years. Probably before you were even born," and he winked. I told him about my mom's close Salvadoran friend who had moved to Washington, DC, because of the civil war.

"Like many of us!" he answered. Just like that, the conversation took a darker turn. He disclosed that he came to Washington, DC, with nothing but his will to live. "I was forced to come to the United States because of the civil war. My family was being hunted down. They killed my family in front of me."

The horrific experiences people faced during the civil wars cannot be overstated. So, when the peace accords were signed in 1987 to establish peace amongst the region's countries, a glimmer of hope sparked—hope that finally people could live peacefully at home.

Oscar Arias, the incumbent President of Costa Rica at the time, led the peace efforts to end the military rule and violence that had reigned in Central America. He heard the cries of Costa Rica's neighboring countries, a region that screamed for help. Through negotiations with the presidents of Honduras, Guatemala, and El Salvador aimed at establishing a strategy to achieve peace in the Central American region, President Arias successfully led the signing of the Esquipulas Peace Accords in 1987. That same year, he received the Nobel Peace Prize.

Theoretically speaking, the signing of the peace accords and the implementation of action steps to cease fire should have ended the violence in these countries. The real question is: did it, really?

Twenty-five years after the signing of the peace accords in Central America, Oscar Arias talked to the *Washington Post* about his role in the historical moment. The signing of the peace accords drew international recognition and showed promise in a troubled region of the world. However, years later, the benefits have yet to come to fruition.[15]

The *Washington Post* described Oscar Arias' dismay at the little progress brought about from the signing of the peace accords: "A quarter-century on, the man of peace still waits. Still waits for the broader hopes of another era to be realized. Still waits for the killing to stop."

Twenty-five years later, as former Costa Rican President Oscar Arias ponders the signing of the Esquipulas accords,

---

15   Manuel Roig-Franzia. "Oscar Arias Sanchez reflects on 25 years since Central American peace accords." *The Washington Post,* August, 2012.

he realizes that the cease-fire that led to the signing of the accords was just an "overture."

As the *Washington Post* described it, "He looks around the region he calls home and sees rampant drug violence, intractable poverty, and too many democratic institutions that seem wobbly and imperiled. Now, he says, instead of mourning young 'guerrilleros'—guerrilla fighters—the region's mothers cry for slain young 'pandilleros'—gang members."[16]

The peace accords should have addressed the structural problems in the countries, stopping future generations of people from leaving their country and preventing the stories of people like Guillermo and Pedro from being repeated.

And yet, the issues that led to the bloody civil wars and military dictatorships have not been solved. They have only been morphed into the same problems with new names. The government entities are not (always) killing their people anymore, but they are still failing to protect their citizens. There are new actors who support violence, such as the infamous gang members. Inequality continues to exist. Getting a decent job is difficult. For this reason, and many others, individuals in Central America continue to leave their countries.

---

16   Manuel Roig-Franzia. "Oscar Arias Sanchez reflects on 25 years since Central American peace accords."

CHAPTER 2

FAMILY FIRST

—

What would you do for your family? To honor your name? How far would you go?

Anastasio Somoza García, also known as "Tacho," took it a little too far. Originally the head of Nicaragua's army, the "Guardia Nacional," in 1933, he soon became power hungry.

With the army at his disposal, he deposed the elected president and assumed office in 1937.[17] That's when Nicaragua's dictatorship started. Although Tacho was not officially the country's president, his position as commander-in-chief guaranteed his rule and his family's rule.

By consolidating his own power, he paved the way for what became a family dynasty, amassing considerable fortune, and taking ownership of large areas of land and many businesses, all in the interest of himself and his family.[18]

---

17 "Somoza Family: Nicaraguan Family," Encyclopedia Brittanica.
18 "Somoza Family: Nicaraguan Family."

Later on, he was succeeded by his son, Luis, as president from 1956 to 1963. Another son, also called Anastasio, succeeded him as head of the National Guard and then as president from 1974 to 1979.[19]

People were increasingly frustrated with the abuses. The Sandinista National Liberation Front (FSLN) developed as a reaction against the dictatorship, through a group of members from civil society, university students, and political activists with a socialist view. Soon enough, they trained guerrilla fighters as part of the movement to counter the dictatorship.

Furthermore, during the Presidency of Anastasio Somoza, Tacho's son, civilians became increasingly vocal against the human rights abuses and repressive measures the family had taken to hush all opposition and consolidate power. In 1978, Pedro Joaquin Chamorro, a newspaper editor and the leader of civilian opposition to the Somoza regime, was assassinated. His relatives later charged the Government with being complicit in the crime, and thus failing to investigate the murder.[20]

The event sparked protests and strikes.

In 1979, while Tacho's son Anastasio was President, the FSLN overthrew him, ending years of a family dynasty, but not without a fight.

---

19 "Somoza Family: Nicaraguan Family."
20 Alan Riding, "Chronic Repression and Corruption Undermine the Somozas' Alliances" The New York Times (Feb 26, 1978).

The Somoza family, through their stubborn need to amass more and more power and repress their opposition, had prompted these reactions from the FSLN and many Nicaraguans in general. For years, the Somozas worked in the interest of their own family—at the expense of other Nicaraguan families. Including my own family.

Carolina, or Caro as I call her, is my mother's first cousin, and she is like another mother to me. She is one of the first people I ever text when I am visiting Costa Rica.

Caro is someone who, like family traditionally does, never misses an opportunity to play a joke on me. While visiting Costa Rica one summer, she told me my legal name was Nemesis Catalina. In my shock that my parents had lied to me all along, I begged her to let me use her phone line to call my parents, who happened to be in Honduras. Meanwhile, she was biting her nails just thinking of the expensive phone bill she was going to get for the little prank she played on me.

I have always loved her and her family dearly (yes, even though she plays pranks on me). I always knew her part of my family fled for their lives from Nicaragua. You would think I would know the details, but despite the joking, the fun times together, and the laughs in between, the exact details of that dark past never came up. The details were an enigma to me until I interviewed Carolina.

It was October of 1978. Caro was only eleven years old and had three siblings.

She recalls having a pleasant life in Nicaragua, with everything a young eleven-year-old girl could ever wish for. She lived in a wonderful house close to the center of Managua, the capital city of Nicaragua. Her parents were also well-off—her dad had studied electrical engineering in the United States and had a job in which he excelled. Despite how content they were, forces outside of their control drove them to leave. Carolina's experience was intertwined with a key moment in the history of the Nicaraguan revolution called *Operación Chanchera* (Operation Chanchera).

Her house was eerily close to the "Bunker," the zone where the military was headquartered, a government building where deputies and other local leaders gathered to make decisions. The National Palace, also in close proximity, was a large building with huge columns and an almost mansion-like look to it. She also knew, despite her young age, that it was the powerhouse of the Nicaraguan government, where the upper-echelon of Nicaraguan society made important decisions.

As part of the events that unfolded during this time, one of the leaders of the revolution, Edén Pastora, also known as "el Comandante Cero" took over the National Palace with a group of guerrilla fighters. He and the guerrilla fighters dressed like the guards that protected the palace, and in an act of trickery, were able to enter the place and disarm the real guards.

The event that followed rattled the country. And it rattled Carolina.

Carolina heard shots fired repeatedly, one sharp blast after another. She instantly diagnosed the proximity of the shots, realizing that they were happening close to her. Shortly after, she was startled by a deafening sound, vibrations that ricocheted through her eardrums; a bomb had exploded. Then another one exploded. Carolina was terrified.

"I was even more terrified because although my dad was there to take care of us, my mom was out in the streets. And I knew she was with my baby brother. I remember my dad picking us up with all his strength, like sacks, and shoving us all of us underneath the bed. Outside, all we could hear was PRARAPAPAPA."

Fortunately, Carolina's baby brother was safe and sound and in the arms of their mother, Mima. Once Mima got home, she decided she would do what was in the best interest of her family. She and her kids would leave immediately.

However, Carolina's dad, Ronnie, had to continue providing for his four children and wife. He stayed in Nicaragua, sending money to his family.

Where Ronnie lived during his remaining stay in Nicaragua resembled a war zone. Neighbors started creating secret passages from one adjacent house to the next as a way of protecting individuals whose homes were being taken over. According to Carolina's recollection of what Ronnie told his family after his experience in what was left of their neighborhood, there were so many bodies scattered throughout the streets that the neighbors burned them. Carolina disclosed that her father never openly admitted to having to burn bodies:

"But deep down, I know he did. And I think it still tears him inside."

After some time, Ronnie decided that it was enough. He joined his family in Costa Rica and started a new life.

The revolution prompted many people to migrate to Costa Rica as well. In the decade from 1990 to 2000, migration to Costa Rica increased by 132 percent. Migration to Costa Rica is prevalent to this day. In 2017, for example, 294,018 Nicaraguans lived in Costa Rica (45 percent of all Nicaraguans living abroad), compared to 275,909 Nicaraguans in the United States (42 percent).[21]

After the revolution, the FSLN became a political party that legitimately won the presidential elections under the leadership of President Daniel Ortega in 1979. After some years of what seemed like democratic rule, things began to go south again. Unfortunately, some good things never last.

Ironically, despite the FSLN's deep rooted stand against the Somoza dictatorship that had ruled in Nicaragua for years and a socialist ideology that promoted equal opportunities to all Nicaraguan families, the party under President Daniel Ortega quickly reversed that stance. He fell into Tacho

---

21 Manuel Orozco, "Country Profile: Nicaragua," *Inter-American Dialogue* (2018: 1).

Somoza's same temptation: the temptation of power. And, like Tacho Somoza, he favored his family over everyone else.

In 2017, he named his own wife, Rosario Murillo, vice-president. Like generations before him, he was only thinking about himself and his family. And once again, it was at the expense of other Nicaraguan families.

In 2018, people began to protest the corrupt electoral system, which was met by violent police repression. It was a mix of many things, among them the fact that President Daniel Ortega, once a symbol of unity to the people, was the antagonist in a regime that has been in power since 2007.

The protests were sparked by a controversial pension reform resolution aimed at stopping the widening deficit in the social security system. The changes increased contributions into the social security system by workers and employers but reduced the pensions of retired workers.[22]

Social security reform was just the straw that broke the camel's back. A series of actions previously taken by Ortega had corroded the integrity of the already weak Nicaraguan institutions, effectively eliminating any checks and balances in place beforehand. In 2009, the Supreme Court granted him the right to run for a second consecutive term, counter to the constitution's stipulations. In 2014, the government backed a change to the constitution, ending term limits.[23]

---

22 Spencer Feingold. "Nicaragua scraps controversial social security reforms." *CNN* (April 2018).

23 Luis Romero. "Since April, more than 300 people have died protesting in Nicaragua. Here's why." *Quartz* (July 2018).

Ortega is in his third consecutive term since 2007.

I have asked many of my Nicaraguan friends who migrated at some point, including my own family, whether they would return to Nicaragua. Many have said no.

After 2018, when the protests were violent enough to kill more than 273 people and injured more than two thousand in clashes between civilians and the national police, many families' prospects of coming back have slimmed down.[24]

Although Nicaragua seems to stand out as a different case than El Salvador, Guatemala, and Honduras due to a different history and waves of out-migration to different destinations, a commonality binds all these countries' experiences: they are countries with historical traumas, weak governance, and large waves of out-migration.

---

24 Kay Guerrero and Theresa Waldrop, "Death toll in Nicaragua protests reaches 273, human rights group says," CNN (July 15, 2018).

CHAPTER 3

THE FACE OF INJUSTICE

When Obispo left his home in Concepción Chiquirichapa in Guatemala, bound for the United States, he followed the tradition of thousands who'd emigrated from Guatemala before him. In 2004, he fled extreme poverty, searching for opportunities elsewhere. What he left behind in his indigenous municipality would soon catch up with him in an unexpected way.

Although Obispo is one of many indigenous people in Guatemala, making up approximately 40 percent of the population, he and his people have been barred from many opportunities—the product of years of systemic abuse dating back to the Spanish conquest and lingering to this day.[25]

Mayan groups, such as the Cakchiquel and the Quiché, resisted the Spanish when they first arrived in Guatemala in 1524. However, a combination of factors, including disease and attacks by the Spanish, contributed to a decline in the

---

25   Verité, "Research on Indicators of Forced Labor in the Supply Chain of Coffee in Guatemala" (2016): 7.

Mayan population. By one estimation, the Mayan population witnessed an 80 percent decrease between 1525 and 1600.[26]

Spanish dominance forced these communities to adapt to the Spanish imperial design, subduing both their land and their labor to the hegemon's whims. The *encomienda* and *repartimiento* systems, for instance, constituted institutional arrangements that granted privileged Spaniards the ability to receive goods and services by the Mayan people, a first step towards their exploitation.[27]

The methods to recruit Mayan workers have differed through the years. President Barrios signed an 1827 law called *mandamiento*, a form of coercion disguised as law that legalized debt peonage and subdued many people to forced labor.[28] In 1934, the signing of a vagrancy law required individuals who held less than a certain amount of land to work part of each year as wage laborers, and most of those affected happened to be indigenous people.[29]

Normalizing these arrangements propagated even more exploitation. As Spanish landowners realized that Verapaz highlands had the perfects conditions to grow coffee, they

---

26 George Lovell, "Surviving Conquest: The Maya of Guatemala in Historical Perspective," *Latin America Research Review*, 1988, Vol. 23, No. 21, pp. 25-57: 29.

27 George Lovell, "Surviving Conquest: The Maya of Guatemala in Historical Perspective," 30.

28 George Lovell, "Surviving Conquest: The Maya of Guatemala in Historical Perspective," 42.

29 George Lovell, "Surviving Conquest: The Maya of Guatemala in Historical Perspective," 42.

acquired them—but needed someone to cultivate the coffee. The Mayan people were perfect candidates.

Static conditions have dragged on through years of exploitation and exclusion.

Not unlike indigenous coffee workers, indigenous people today represent 50 percent of the agricultural workforce.[30] Although everyone in this sector faces exploitation, indigenous people have it worse.

In 2018, the coffee sector represented the second greatest export commodity in the country, totaling $775 million worth of exports. According to studies by the non-governmental organization (NGO) Global Exchange, Guatemalan coffee workers' average income totaled $127 per month, whereas the basic food basket cost amounts to $171 per month. A basket that includes education, health care, clothing, and transportation costs $313 per month. According to the same NGO report, Guatemalan coffee workers must pick a one-hundred-pound quota to earn the legally required minimum of four dollars per day, and they are frequently forced to work overtime without compensation.[31]

Despite the widespread abuse of all coffee workers, indigenous people face greater discrimination. A survey of coffee workers by Verité found that 47.8 percent of non-indigenous

---

30 Verité, "Research on Indicators of Forced Labor in the Supply Chain of Coffee in Guatemala" (2016): 50.

31 Elliot J. Schrage, *Promoting International Worker Rights through Private Voluntary Initiatives.*Iowa: The UI Center for Human Rights, *The University of Iowa: Center for Human Rights.* 2004. Web. 6 Apr. 2017: 76

reported that they did not earn enough to pay their expenses and debts, compared to 61 percent of interviewed indigenous workers. In addition, 11.3 percent of indigenous workers interviewed reported having suffered discrimination, compared to 2.2 percent of non-indigenous.[32]

Did the independence of Guatemala in 1821 equal freedom for indigenous people too? Nearly two centuries of human rights violations indicate otherwise.

Years after independence, the military regimes of Romeo Lucas García, Efraín Ríos Montt, and Oscar Mejía Víctores claimed the lives of thousands of Mayans.[33]

In 2015, while reading the news, my eyes raced to a headline that disturbed me. Ríos Montt would not go to trial because a psychological evaluation found that he suffered from vascular dementia, making him incapable of confronting a judge. During Rios Montt's military mandate from 1982 to 1983, he led a genocide that attempted to exterminate the Ixil ethnic group, ordering the murder of 771 people who died at the hands of the military he led.[34]

In 1982, the year Ríos Montt came to power, a witness gave his account of a horrible military attack in Finca San Francisco,

32 Verité, "Research on Indicators of Forced Labor in the Supply Chain of Coffee in Guatemala" (2016): 50.

33 George Lovell, "Surviving Conquest: The Maya of Guatemala in Historical Perspective," 45.

34 Jerson Ramos y Acan - Efe, "Efraín Ríos Montt padece demencia vascular," *Prensa Libre*, August 18, 2015.

a remote settlement in the Department of Huehuetenango, near the border with Mexico:

"Soldiers took our wives out of the church in groups of ten or twenty. Then twelve or thirteen soldiers went into our houses to rape our wives. After they were finished raping them, they shot our wives and burned the houses down. All of our children had been left locked up in the church."[35]

In 2019, the military covertly killed several Guatemalan indigenous activists, raising the issue of human rights violations similar to those experienced during the civil war. One of the victims, Juana Raymundo, a 25-year-old Ixil Maya nurse and recently elected leader of an indigenous civic committee, suffered the consequences of an unjust state. One day, while delivering paperwork for her job, she disappeared. Days later, her body appeared in a river covered by brush.[36] She is just one of the many cases.

Jim Crow laws, enacted in post–Civil War United States and lasting until 1968, affected Black people's livelihood in the segregated South. Requisites like literacy tests and arbitrary trials, like the "jelly bean test" that required Black voters to guess the number of beans in a jar, were tools for racial discrimination.[37] These laws, under the guise of justice, only further disenfranchised Black people. In Guatemala, a

---

35 George Lovell, "Surviving Conquest: The Maya of Guatemala in Historical Perspective," 46.

36 Maria Martin, "Killings of Guatemala's Indigenous Activists Raise Specter of Human Rights Crisis." All Things Considered, *NPR,* January 22, 2019.

37 The Associated Press, "Exhibit traces history of Voting Rights Act," NBC News, 2005.

similar tactic excluded indigenous women. With the democratic revolution in Guatemala from 1944 to 1954, progressive laws allowed women to vote for the first time. However, a prerequisite excluded most indigenous women: they had to know how to write and read. Given the many languages spoken in Guatemala, the restriction naturally prohibited the majority of indigenous women from the right to vote.[38]

Little things, like the language barrier that Spanish represents for indigenous people, are just some of the mechanisms through which they are systematically excluded.

The language barrier certainly excluded and isolated Obispo.

Before coming to the United States, Obispo had never learned grammar: "The exclamation mark, the question mark, comma, period, all of that, I didn't know how to use it. I also didn't have good vocabulary. Something as simple as that. My overall lack of education impeded me from writing."

In fact, when Obispo moved to the United States, he barely spoke any Spanish and spoke no English, only Mam, a Mayan language. This language barrier and overall lack of education that had made him an outsider in his own country also made him an outsider in the United States when he migrated.

Despite his lack of education, his dream was to become a poet.

---

38 Ana Lorena Carrillo, "Indias y Ladinas: Los Ásperos Caminos de las Mujeres en Guatemala," in *Antología del pensamiento crítico guatemalteco contemporáneo,* ed. Guillermo Toriello et al. (Buenos Aires: CLACSO, 2019), 618.

In the United States, he caught up on years of lack of education. His dreams came to fruition when he found an organization called CENAES (Alphabetization Center), where he learned how to read and write Spanish.

While taking classes at CENAES, he met two Colombian teachers who were like angels in his life. Not only did they help him speak Spanish as well as he does today, they also motivated him to take the first leap into his poetry-writing journey.

"I told them how badly I wanted to write poetry. But that I didn't have the tools because of my lack of education. The teachers emphasized that, if I put the hard work, with time I would see progress. And soon enough I did."

After his first poem, dedicated to his mother, he began to write other pieces until a local newspaper, Tiempo Latino from Silver Spring, Maryland featured him on the front page. Then he had an interview on the radio.

He achieved another dream: doing a poetry reading in a theater. His friend contacted a venue, Teatro de la Luna, on Georgia Avenue in Washington, DC. They called him back.

"I felt ecstatic. To know that people, poets, and those involved in the literary world enjoyed my writing, appreciated my words. What an amazing feeling."

After the poetry reading, Univision, a very important US-based Spanish-language television network, featured him in a short documentary.

Despite his success today, his journey has not always been that easy.

His poems depict his experiences as an indigenous person living in Guatemala: inaccessible education, unequal rights, and an exclusionary government.

"The government is damaging the Earth," he explained, "contaminating it and destroying it. We can't even cultivate crops anymore."

Often the poems represent how his people, the indigenous community, have been excluded and abused through years. "Mi pueblo ha sido humillado." My people have been humiliated.

"Ultimately, I write about the suffering of people, my people who are ignored, whose rights are violated because, just by not writing and speaking Spanish, they are taken advantage of. More than anything, my poems are about injustice."

In the United States, he also faces discrimination. He confessed he isn't the only one: "Many indigenous Guatemalans come to the United States and face similar struggles I did, adapting while speaking neither Spanish nor English. We face discrimination here too."

Lastly, he expressed sadness that his government never appreciated the beauty of his language and his community, never granting him the opportunity at home to exploit his creative mind and love for poetry in his mother tongue.

In line with this notion, he explained that the poem he is currently working on is about migration and the struggles involved.

Guatemala's indigenous population is prevalent, explaining why 41 percent of Guatemalans who migrate come from indigenous communities, compared to 0.2 percent for El Salvador and 7.2 percent in Honduras.[39] Obispo is just one of many who, in the face of injustice, decided to take a leap of faith and leave everything behind.

---

39 Emmanuel Abuelafia, Giselle Del Carmen, Marta Ruiz-Arranz, "Tras los pasos del migrante: Perspectivas y experiencias de la migración de El Salvador, Guatemala y Honduras en Estados Unidos," *Inter-American Development Bank* (December 2019: 8).

CHAPTER 4

THE ABANDONED YOUTH

———

I grew up fearing the *maras*.

Maras are gangs formed by youth who have inevitably become antagonists in Central America. I watched documentaries and listened to stories of the treacherous things *mareros* (gang members) would do to their victims—how they would cut heads off and play soccer with them. I heard about how their rite of passage was to pick a random car and kill everyone inside, a sign of loyalty to the gang sealed with blood. They were trained to find normalcy in death.

I was always terrified of what seemed like a cult to me, so much so that they would mark themselves with tattoos.

The tattoos were different depending on the gang, but amongst the most common ones included the spiderweb, a variety of religious symbols including the image of Jesus, and even the yin-yang symbol. The spiderweb, for instance, represents the gangs' expansion of power. The yin-yang, on the other hand, is used as an expression of going beyond traditional understandings of the balance between good and evil—through violence and death.[40]

In recent years, gangs have ceased to use tattoos as a symbol of membership to their respective gang, a strategic decision to evade justice.[41] However, by the time I was a young adult, that trauma had been ingrained in my mind. By then, I had already seen too many images of detained *mareros*: shirtless guys with tattoos splattered throughout their entire body and face, doing strange symbols with their hands, proud of the pain they had caused.

Despite being antagonists throughout the Central American countries, the truth is that *maras* were born from war, from migration, from deportation, and, most importantly, from negligence.

Many Salvadorans moved to different parts of the United States, some of them fleeing for their lives. From 1970 to 1990, the population of El Salvadorans in the United States exploded.[42]

Many of these people weren't just migrants. They were refugees. They were asylum seekers. However, despite the

---

40 James Bargent, "Explicación de los significados ocultos de los tatuajes de las maras de Honduras," *InSightCrime,* September 3, 2014.

41 Angélica Gallón, "La estratégica razón por la que ahora la MS-13 prohíbe a sus miembros llevar tatuajes," *Univisión Noticias,* March 18, 2018.

42 Cecilia Menjívar and Andrea Gómez Cervantes, "El Salvador: Civil War, Natural Disasters, and Gang Violence Drive Migration," *Migration Policy Institute,* (August 29, 2018)

common knowledge that a war was going on in El Salvador, the US authorities were not lenient with incoming Salvadorans. In the 1980s, only 2 percent of asylum applications were approved.[43] The unfair treatment of Salvadoran and Guatemalan asylum seekers was raised by a group of religious organizations and refugee advocacy organizations. In 1991, the "ABC Settlement Agreement" was settled after these organizations filed a lawsuit against the government. Through the agreement, the Immigration Naturalization Services (INS), now called US Citizenship and Immigration Services, had to hold asylum hearings under new and fair regulations, unlike those in the 1980s.[44]

Unfortunately, by the time the agreement was passed, and Salvadoran asylum seekers were treated more fairly, many youth had suffered irreparable damage. Without legal documents in a country that is unforgiving to undocumented people, young Salvadorans had limited opportunities. Integration became almost impossible.

A major gang, the 18th Street gang, named after 18th Street in Los Angeles, formed in the 1960s by Mexican youth who had not been accepted into existing Hispanic gangs. When Salvadorans started migrating to Los Angeles, the 18th Street gang began recruiting them.[45] Salvadorans in Los Angeles

43 Sarah Gammage, "El Salvador: Despite End to Civil War, Emigration Continues," *Migration Policy Institute,* (July 26, 2007).
44 Sarah Gammage, "El Salvador: Despite End to Civil War, Emigration Continues."
45 Clare Ribando Seelke, "Gangs in Central America," Congressional Research Service (2016): 3

soon created their own rival gang in the 1980s: MS-13, also known as *Mara Salvatrucha*.[46]

The real issues for Central America started when the United States began deporting undocumented immigrants back to their country, facilitated by the Illegal Immigrant Reform and Immigrant Responsibility Act (IIRIRA; P.L. 104-208) of 1996, an act that expanded the categories of undocumented immigrants subject to deportation, many of whom, by then, had been recruited by gangs.[47]

The US government returned young Salvadorans to a country in the midst of post-civil war reconstruction, a state that did not prioritize helping deportees reintegrate into society. The youths appropriated many attitudes of the MS-13 and 18th Street gangs.[48] That's how *maras* began to terrorize first El Salvador, then Honduras and Guatemala, and eventually most of Central America. Essentially, the issue of gangs was transferred from the hands of the United States, to the hands of institutionally weak governments.

How did Central American governments cope with *maras*? With Mano Dura.

"Mano Dura" means Iron-Fist in Spanish, an allusion to the exercise of power in an oppressive or ruthless way. I was eight years old and living in Honduras when I first heard the term on television. Honduras' president, Ricardo Maduro, went

---

46   Clare Ribando Seelke, "Gangs in Central America": 3
47   Clare Ribando Seelke, "Gangs in Central America": 3
48   José Miguel Cruz, "Central American *maras*: from youth street gangs to transnational protection rackets," *Global Crime* 11, no. 4 (2010): 379-398.

on TV one morning and used the term to describe the new approach that the country would adopt to eradicate gangs. To me, a young girl who knew nothing of public policy or politics, the coined word was reminiscent of a parent's approach to punishment that involved harsh and oppressive measures. Despite being so young, my analogy was not too far off from the suggested approach.

Mano Dura policies first began in El Salvador and quickly spread to Honduras and Guatemala, where gang violence was rampant. On July 23, 2003, El Salvador's incumbent president, Francisco Flores, declared the Mano Dura plan with the objective of curbing gang power and reducing homicide rates. The approach fixated on law enforcement and widespread incarceration of youth associated with gangs, putting fourteen thousand youth behind bars between 2004 and 2005.[49] In addition, the incumbent president introduced the Ley Anti-Maras (Anti-Gang Law) as a six-month emergency measure to address gang violence.[50]

Despite these efforts, the approach proved futile. The increase in homicide rates is one of the greatest paradoxes that Mano Dura proponents have been forced to face. In 2003, the homicide rate was 36.4 percent as compared to 69.9 percent in 2011, after Mano Dura policies were at its highest peak.[51]

---

49 U.S. Law Library of Congress, The United States Department of Justice, El Salvador: Gang Violence, by Norma C. Gutiérrez, 008435 (2012), 2.

50 U.S. Law Library of Congress, (2012), 2.

51 Carlos A. Carballo, "El Salvadors crime prevention policies from Mano Dura to El Salvador Seguro," *Calhoun: The NPS Institutional Archive* (2015): 10.

A report by the Center of Hemispheric Policy from the University of Miami summarizes the aftermath of the advances we have seen after the implementation of these approaches in El Salvador, Honduras, and Guatemala. Not only does the report suggest that violent crime levels have remained high in all three countries, but many of the youth that had been arrested during the Mano Dura mandates have been released due to the lack of evidence that they committed any crime at all. Just in El Salvador, more than ten thousand of the fourteen thousand suspected gang members arrested in 2005 were later released.[52]

The wrongful conviction of young people into overcrowded prisons backfired. Many people were incarcerated without substantiated evidence against them. Those people who otherwise would not have joined a gang were actually recruited in prisons. In short, many young people entered the prison as honest people and left the prison as gang members.

Decades after the US passed the gang problem to Central America then washed its hands of the consequences, the problem made its way back to the blood-stained hands of the US government. In Suffolk County, Long Island, the MS-13 gang was blamed for seventeen of forty-five murders between January 2016 and May 2017.[53] In the Greater Washington, DC,

---

52 U.S. Library of Congress. Congressional Research Service. Anti-Gang Efforts in Central America: Moving Beyond the Mano Dura? by Clare Ribando Seelke (2007), 3.

53 Steven Dudley and Héctor Silva Ávalos, "MS13 in the Americas: How the World's Most Notorious Gang Defies Logic, Resists Destruction," *InSite Crime* and *Center for Latin American & Latino Studies,* February 16, 2018.

area, there are less homicides linked to MS-13, but when they do murder, they do so brutally and in a macabre fashion.[54]

The Trump administration has made the gang a top priority, placing enforcement resources towards this end. In the process, the administration has used the gang for political purposes, conflating the dangers of undocumented migrants with gang violence to further his anti-immigration agenda.

However, continuing to deport people, as we have learned, only makes the problem worse. It has all become a vicious cycle that leads to the continued out-flow of migrants from the region. There were civil wars that, due to violence, led many people to flee. And when these people were deported back to their respective countries, they were given no economic opportunities or support to reintegrate into society. These young people became the seed of continued violence, and that violence continues to push people out. They are different actors who cause similar problems.

Migration flows continue not only to the United States, but to other destinations, such as Europe.

Melissa Vida is an LA-born Salvadoran and Belgian. She is currently an editor, a freelance journalist, and speaker with bylines in the *New York Times*, *Foreign Policy*, *NACLA*, and *El Faro*. As someone with both Central American and European origins, most of her work has focused on making Central American known to Europe and to the world. In the process,

---

54   Steven Dudley and Héctor Silva Ávalos, "MS13 in the Americas: How the World's Most Notorious Gang Defies Logic, Resists Destruction."

she has become a kind of bridge between both regions, particularly between Belgium and El Salvador.

Melissa spoke at a conference organized by the state agency in charge of hosting refugees in Belgium, where many social workers gathered and exchanged ideas about the wave of migration coming from El Salvador.

According to FFM, a German nonprofit that focuses on migration and migration policy, the number of Central Americans seeking asylum in Europe has increased nearly 4,000 percent in the last decade. In 2018, a total of 7,800 people applied for asylum in Europe, up from 4,835 in 2017—a 61 percent increase.[55] As of 2019, Belgium is the third main destination country behind Spain and Italy, and among the top ten countries with highest asylum applicants in 2019.[56]

While Melissa was at the conference, many of the social workers expressed to her how unprepared they felt receiving Salvadoran migrants: "One lady came up to me and said that she knew how to speak Pashto and Arabic...but not Spanish!"

During the conference, Melissa gave her speech on the topic of Salvadoran migrants in Belgium. She was approached by people representing anti-terrorist organizations, investigative police officers, and people who were simply curious, with a range of inquiries. One question kept coming up again and

---

55 "For Central Americans, Fleeing to Europe May Beat Trying to Reach U.S," Forschungsgesellschaft Flucht und Migration eV (2019). Accessed, May 10, 2020.

56 Daniel Boffey, "As Trump closes US doors to migrants, Latin Americans look to Europe," *The Guardian*, July 10, 2019.

again: "Melissa…Do you think gang members will try to infiltrate into Belgium?"

Melissa wasn't surprised with the question in the context of Europe, a region terrified of the threat infiltrated jihadists represent. If they were dangerous, weren't the Salvadorans dangerous too?

She quickly realized how important her take was on this question and how her response could elicit many people's opinion on policies aimed at supporting Salvadoran migrants.

"Anything is possible. There may be gang members, both active and inactive ones, coming to plead for asylum. But… do they have to continue their illicit activities here if they have food and housing and are taken care of? A lot of gang formations stem from the poverty and marginalization that has happened for years in our country. Part of it is also a desire to be part of something, like a clan.

So, if these men come here, and are broken away from their networks, do they have to kill to steal if they have food? Things like this happened in the US in the 90s because these kids were completely abandoned. On top of that, the United States provided no state support at all because the US did not recognize Salvadorans entering the country as refugees, even if they were coming because of a civil war. So delinquent clans were forming in the streets, particularly in LA."

Melissa warned us of the potential downfalls of failing to categorize Salvadoran or Central American individuals with legitimate claims for asylum as what they actually are:

refugees. Unfortunately, the United States seems not to learn from past mistakes.

Vanessa Leandro is a lawyer from Costa Rica who worked for the United Nations High Commissioner for Refugees (UNHCR) in San José for many years. "To this day, the topic of refugees is one that I am passionate about." She says that a woman who worked at the UNHCR had suggested she apply, but at the time Vanessa worked as a smaller law firm that protected migrants at the border.

"I went to the Nicaragua and Costa Rican border all the time, meeting people, helping them out, listening to their stories. It was so fulfilling and hard at the same time."

After years of working with UNHCR, she has become well acquainted with who can apply for refugee status based on the United Nations Convention Relating to the Status of Refugees, ratified in 1951 by 145 state parties. According to the convention, a refugee "is someone who is unable or unwilling to return to their country of origin owing to a well-founded fear of being persecuted for reasons of race, religion, nationality, membership of a particular social group, or political opinion."[57]

In Costa Rica, Vanessa explained, the two most cited reasons for granting refugee status include one's membership of a particular social group or one's political opinion.

---

57 *Convention and Protocol Relating to the Status of Refugees.* 1951 Convention, Resolution 2198 (XXI) adopted by the United Nations General Assembly. United Nations High Commissioner for Refugees.

"To be categorized as a refugee based on political opinion, you don't have to necessarily be a politician or a well-known activist," Vanessa explained. While we spoke, she provided the following example: a dentist with a dental office has a permit issued by the state to work there. Maybe the dentist goes on a public demonstration one day and, as a result, the permit is revoked by the state. That can already count as persecution for political opinion.

Under the stipulated convention, violence or persecution from gangs or other criminal organizations is also a valid reason to seek asylum. It also includes other categories, such as people from the LGBTQ community facing persecution, gender-based violence, and others. "The 1951 Convention provides great flexibility."

She also explained that the UNHCR does not use the term failing states or weak states because it is a political and diplomatic organization. But she knows that any UNHCR office will do their due diligence and find out about each country's context. "Some states have failed to protect people. We see this particularly in Central American countries and Venezuela. It implies that, for many, the legal system has failed them somehow. So we are more accepting of those cases."

The most shocking fact I learned from Vanessa is that basically every country in the world ratified the Convention—except for the United States and Cuba.

The US has its own version of the Convention through Temporary Protected Status (TPS) granted to people who are in the following situations: situations of armed violence and conflict, natural disaster or an epidemic, or other extraordinary and temporary conditions. The last option provides certain flexibility but is at the discretion of the officials. Furthermore, even those granted TPS status face hardships to adapt to the country.

Brenda perched her head on the airplane's window, observing the heavy rain fall against the midnight sky. It was December 1998, and she was only three years old when she flew to Los Angeles with her mother and sister, where her aunt lived. They were from Santiago Texacuangos, an area that, like the rest of El Salvador, had been consumed by years of war and hardships, allowing them to apply for TPS status in the United States. After arriving at their aunt's place, Brenda and her family slept on the cold floor of the garage. It was the start of something new, but it wouldn't be easy for them.

"There was a lot of stress linked to having TPS. For one, it is very expensive to maintain that status. My family had to budget approximately two thousand dollars a year to pay for the status, while earning five dollars an hour at work. Meanwhile, we sent approximately four hundred dollars a month to our grandparents. For us, it was a lot."

Brenda's father joined the rest of the family later on and worked several jobs to generate income but staying afloat was hard. "Luckily, we always got support from the church—we got food baskets, donations, clothes. Sometimes I wore boy clothes because that's what they had sent!"

In addition to the economic burden, the stress of constantly renewing TPS added to their burdens. "Since I was in elementary school, I was always nervous about my status. I always thought I would get screwed over. I knew my parents were worried about renewing it, and not missing the deadlines." Until she finally gained citizenship, Brenda confessed to feeling disenfranchised in the country where she grew up.

"I became a citizen in 2018. It wasn't until then that my family and I felt empowered—eighteen years after arriving. TPS allowed us to stay, but not to feel like we belonged. Tomorrow night, they want to discuss the California ballot propositions, which is something that I would never expect to be talking about with them. I know that a lot of my friends and their parents still feel like outsiders because their vote doesn't count."

Despite the struggles associated with TPS, Brenda is thankful that she and her family had it. "TPS was a blessing for us—it allowed my mother to work several jobs. It allowed her to work as a babysitter at first. And then it allowed her to work at a clinic where she increased in rank throughout the years. I feel very fortunate that we had that status."

The United States should rethink asylum from Central America by granting asylum officers the ability to make a final decision on asylum, paired with credible-fear screenings, as per the recommendation of policy experts at the Migration Policy Institute. This approach is less expensive than the system in place and allows for faster processing.[58] However,

---

58   Andrew Selee, Silvia E. Giorguli-Saucedo, Claudia Masferrer, and Ariel G. Ruiz Soto, "Strategic Solutions for the United States and Mexico to Manage the Migration Crisis," *Migration Policy Institute*, (July 2019).

the current system is far from following this advice—quite the opposite.

Sweeping anti-immigrant policy changes stripped protections away from refugee seekers, denying safety afforded to them by TPS, causing even more harm to this vulnerable population. With the stroke of a pen, President Trump and then Attorney General Jeff Sessions eliminated gang and domestic violence as reasons to grant protection. Furthermore, they issued a rule that required migrants to seek and be denied asylum in a first country of transit before requesting asylum in the United States, a rule that quickly faced legal challenge and which the UNHCR denounced as a threat to vulnerable people.[59]

In September 2020, a federal appeals court decision brought the Trump administration forward with plans to terminate TPS for three hundred thousand immigrants from El Salvador, Haiti, Nicaragua, and Sudan. This would force them to return to their countries despite holding legal status. Many of them, like Brenda's parents before earning citizenship, have lived in the United States for decades.[60]

Meanwhile, people continue facing violence at home and seeking help in the United States and other countries. Surveys from the US Citizenship and Immigration Services in

---

59 Andrew Selee, Silvia E. Giorguli-Saucedo, Claudia Masferrer, and Ariel G. Ruiz Soto, "Strategic Solutions for the United States and Mexico to Manage the Migration Crisis."

60 Jacqueline Charles, David Smiley, Monique Madan, "Federal appeals court decision brings Trump administration closer to ending TPS," *Miami Herald*, September 14, 2020.

2018 shows that 76 percent of individuals interviewed who were requesting asylum (the majority being Central American) showed signs of credible fear.[61]

Central American history taught us how counterproductive and detrimental deportations can be. It was detrimental to Central American countries that were trying to get on their feet. And now, it is part of the reason why the US continues receiving large waves of migration.

If only a more inclusive approach had been used to support migrants in the first place, to provide asylum to those in need of protection, providing quicker legal pathways to live in the United States, integration might have been easier. Perhaps Brenda's family might have adapted quicker. Perhaps I would not have developed the aversion I had toward tattoos. And more importantly, the abandoned youth might not have used tattoos as a symbol of unity to a group that promotes violence and death.

It took me a while to get over the symbolic link between gangs and tattoos. It wasn't until I moved to DC and met my partner, someone with so many tattoos I have lost count (ink on the chest, arms, legs, and back) that I realized how irrational my feelings toward tattoos were. I have gotten over my fear of tattoos, especially when I think of the difficult reality that the youth in gangs have lived.

---

61 Doris Meissner, Faye Hipsman, T. Alexander Aleinikoff, "The U.S. Asylum System in Crisis: Charting a Way Forward," *Migration Policy Institute*, 2018: 18.

The religious symbols and the yin-yang symbol many *mare-ros* have is not unlike one of the tattoos my partner has across his chest—a virgin and a rosary close-framing the phrase "Obey thy heart," a symbol for the balance between good (represented by the virgin) and evil, and the ability to choose correctly, although sometimes your choice might not be the right one. They are similar because they represent that balance. However, in the case of *maras*, their balance is tipped toward evil.

And yet, perhaps they never wanted to be part of the gang, being forcefully recruited or joining because they had no options in a world that had abandoned them.

In fact, one of the tattoos *maras* used years ago was two hands clasped in prayer, implying regret for the things they have done, but recognition that they cannot leave behind the gang life or they risk retaliation.[62] Once they join, they can never leave.

For the abandoned youth of the 80s, and of generations later, it is too late. Many youths have joined gangs, and quitting is difficult, sometimes impossible. The least governments can do, both in Central America and destination countries, is not repeat the same mistakes, so that youth are never abandoned again.

---

62 James Bargent, "Explicación de los significados ocultos de los tatuajes de las maras de Honduras."

PART II

WHAT IS GOING ON IN CENTRAL AMERICA?

CHAPTER 5

WHEN THE RISK IS WORTH THE JOURNEY

———

The pastor found her sprawled across the floor, unconscious. She appeared to be a teenager—not yet eighteen—and, from the looks of her sunburned skin, she had taken a long, hot journey to end up in his path, just north of the US-Mexico border.

He slowly knelt for a closer look at the young woman's condition. She was dehydrated. She was alone. She was pregnant.

Earlier that day, she had crossed the border with six other Central Americans. Hungry, thirsty, and weary from walking for almost a week, they'd followed their guide—called a coyote—up the front steps of a family's home.

As they stood in the doorway, asking the American family for help, their would-be rescuers instead released two blood-thirsty dogs, one black and one brown one, that began hunting them down.

Everyone branched into different directions, losing sight of their peers. Norma, a seventeen-year-old woman from Honduras, looked over her shoulder just as one of the dogs violently bit a Salvadoran in the group. She sprinted uncontrollably until she found a place she thought was safe. She prayed and then fainted.

Minutes later, like a prayer answered, he was there by her side—the pastor.

When Norma woke up, she was in his house. Her head was spinning as she looked around and was unable to recognize where she was. When the pastor appeared, the first words she uttered were, "Agua, agua." He quickly gave her water and food.

Thanks to the pastor, she survived, and was able to start a new life in San Antonio, Texas. She became one of the 354,000 Central Americans in the US in the 1980s.[63]

Not everyone in her group made it. In fact, as they crossed the US-Mexico border, many of the people in her group were lost along the way.

In July of 1988, she met up with the coyote in a ranch in Mexico where there were approximately fifteen people, mostly from Honduras, Guatemala, and El Salvador. The days before, she had been planning the logistics of her trip: finding a coyote, coordinating with her aunt who lived in San Antonio,

---

63   Jie Zong and Jeanne Batalova, "Central American Immigrants in the United States in 2013," *Migration Policy Institute* (September 2015).

finding someone to drive her all the way to Mexico. The first part of the trip was easy. The rest was a nightmare.

Norma walked for hours, and then days. Restlessness was in the air, tensions building as Norma and the others wondered how much longer they had to walk.

A Guatemalan man in the pack, frustrated at how long they had been walking, confronted the coyote: "You have no idea where we are going, do you? We keep walking and walking, like we are going in circles."

Norma was equally frustrated. It was July, and she felt the scorching, midsummer heat against her back. Her pregnancy made her particularly susceptible to pain, and her feet were swollen.

"I cannot believe we are all going to die because of you, because you have no idea where you are taking us. This is your fault!" the Guatemalan fired up again, yelling and cursing at the coyote. Quickly, his fury escalated from yelling to pushing the coyote. Then the Guatemalan man jumped on top of him, throwing the first punch.

Dust levitated off the ground as they rolled around, punching and grunting and attacking each other with the little energy they still had.

Someone in the group gasped loudly, just as Norma noticed the coyote had drawn his gun from his waistband and smacked the Guatemalan on his head—rendering him unconscious. They all witnessed as the coyote stood, straightened his shirt and put the gun back into his waistband.

"Let's keep going," he said, unfazed by what he had just done. Unlike the Guatemalan man, Norma did not complain. She kept walking. And walking. And walking.

That's how they went from fifteen to fourteen people.

It wasn't long before the group would sustain two more casualties. A couple from Puerto Cortés, Honduras—the wife, nearly full-term in her pregnancy—struggled to keep up with the others. "Her legs were swollen. She was also itching because we were all full of bites, even tick bites. Her husband told her that he would help her through it, that she could make it. But two hours in, she sat down and said she couldn't keep going. She was severely dehydrated…so we had to leave them there."

Along the way, more people were lost. At some point, Norma realized she had been walking for three days straight. And then four days. And then five days. Until, as if waking up from a frenzy, she realized only six people were left. They had no food and no water. That's what led them to the Americans' house, where they were chased down by dogs.

Norma's journey, a journey that happened in 1988, is all too common even today. Years later, migration has not ceased. If anything, it has multiplied.

From 1980 to 2013, the size of the Central American immigration population grew nine-fold. Just in 2013, approximately

3.2 million Central American immigrants resided in the United States—the majority from the Northern Triangle countries of El Salvador, Guatemala, and Honduras.[64] This represents 7 percent of the 41.3 million immigrants in the US.

Thirty-two years after Norma left, in the middle of a country where peace had not yet been achieved, people are still leaving in masses, sometimes using migrant caravans.

The first reported migrant caravan left in October of 2018 from San Pedro Sula, one of Honduras' main cities, with approximately 160 people. The caravan traveled through the territories of three Central American countries: Honduras, Guatemala, and El Salvador. After 2,500 miles (4,000 km) of travel, 1,500 migrants had reached Tijuana, Mexico.[65]

The migrant caravan was a grass-roots effort started through social media. Eventually, it was popularized and almost everyone throughout Central America knew about it.

Think about it—would you pick up everything and jump on a caravan that you heard about through Facebook?

Jeff Ernst witnessed firsthand the desperation and urgency with which people were willing to leave their country and hop on that caravan. Originally from Minnesota, Jeff has a great admiration for Central America. His interest in the

---

64   Jie Zong and Jeanne Batalova, "Central American Immigrants in the United States in 2013."

65   "Migrant caravan: What is it and why does it matter?" *BBC News* (November 2018).

region stems from his grandfather, who, since the 70s, had been volunteering for medical brigades in isolated areas.

Because of his grandfather's connection to Honduras, Jeff traveled there often: "I went down as a kid and then started going down after high school as much as possible. It's just kind of been a second home for me."

Years later, his admiration for the country lives on. Jeff is now a freelance investigative journalist covering a variety of topics on Central America, such as corruption and migration. Although he is based in Honduras, he travels around the Central American region in his car, talking to a myriad of people along the way. Right before the COVID-19 lockdown, Jeff was traveling throughout Nicaragua when the pandemic was announced. He knew he couldn't keep driving his car in the midst of a pandemic; he was scared of borders being closed down. Without many more options, he decided to leave his car in Nicaragua and take a plane to his family in Minnesota. He says, "If it weren't for the pandemic progressing so quickly, I would have driven all the way from Nicaragua to Minnesota. I've done that before!"

On one of his many travels throughout Central America, Jeff had the opportunity to speak and interact with some of the migrants in the first infamous caravan that departed from Honduras to the United States in 2018.

"Regarding the profile of individuals who were joining the caravans, they were actually not the nuts-and-bolts of the poor. You know, they're the people that could be considered middle class oftentimes. And these are often people who *tried* to make a living at home."

Jeff recalled that one of the most shocking discoveries while talking to some of these migrants was how sudden the decision to leave had been.

"What was most remarkable for me while interviewing people, especially in the first caravan, is they didn't have plans!"

Jeff told me about one such family from Honduras. They heard the caravan was coming through their town and didn't hesitate to join.

"They were eating, and still had food on the table…and they just left."

What's more surprising is that he wasn't the only one. Thousands of people made this decision, knowing that there could be dire consequences. The stakes were extremely high.

"Originally, it looked like a great new innovation in mobility that'll help migrants without having to pay for a coyote or worry about being preyed on," Andrew Selee, President of Migration Policy Institute commented.[66] The hope was that by banding together in a larger caravan with a larger group of people, migrants would be more protected from some of the dangers often faced in the trajectory up North, such as kidnappings and gang violence. Despite the original intention

---

66 Priscilla Alvarez. "What happened to the migrant caravans?" *CNN* (March 2019).

of the caravan to improve the conditions for these migrants, the outcomes were not as rosy.

Migrants faced many adversities along the way. At the Guatemala-Mexico border, border agents crippled them in a fog of tear gas that burned their eyes and left them gasping for air. Once they reached Tijuana, rioters holding up signs reading "no to the invasion" challenged them.[67] In addition, President Donald Trump ordered a massive military deployment at the border to keep these migrants from entering. Once they reached Tijuana, they had to make the decision of whether or not to ask for asylum in the United States, something they are entitled to request, according to international law, if they are facing persecution in their home country. But, that process is not always well-accepted in the United States, even for people with legitimate claims for asylum.

What happened to the family who risked everything to go North?

"They actually made it!" Jeff happily told me. "I'm so glad he made it. He just seemed like the kind of person who really deserved that."

Not everyone was as fortunate. Throughout the trajectory, the number of migrants in the caravan peaked at more than 7,000 at one point. While some stayed along the way, others faced adversities, such as the aforementioned ones, that made it impossible for them to continue. When the caravan arrived in Tijuana, only 1,500 migrants remained.

---

67   "Migrant caravan: What is it and why does it matter?"

Because of the continuous waves of migration, the topic has become a top priority, both in the United States as well as Central American countries.

A 2019 Gallup study showed that 23 percent of Americans cite "immigration" as the most important problem facing the country, falling closely behind "the government" at 26 percent. Never before in Gallup's twenty-seven-year recorded history of collecting data on immigration had the public's concern about immigration issues been so great.[68]

Governments in Central America persistently address the topic of migration, especially after the migrant caravan. Approximately a year ago, I was in Honduras watching TV when the first lady, Ana García de Hernandez, spoke about the dangers of the caravan journey in an effort to disincentivize people from joining. A similar urgency is seen in Guatemala. Even before taking the position of incumbent President of Guatemala in January 2020, Alejandro Giammattei had already been summoned by US Secretary of State, Mike Pompeo, in August to speak about the issue of migration.[69]

Despite this urgency to address the topic, these issues have existed for much longer, since Norma left in 1988 and even before. Perhaps this is the first sign that something is wrong. With how consistently people have been leaving, how might

---

68 Jeffrey Jones, "New High in US Say Immigration Most Important Problem," *Gallup* (June 2019).
69 David Alandete, "Alejandro Giammattei: Admito que Guatemala es un problema de seguridad para Estados Unidos," *ABC Internacional* (September 2019).

this be an indicator of unresolved structural issues lurking in the background?

While politicians sit in their offices and discuss how to address the topic, the people receive the hit and are involved in the physical act of moving from one country to the next. As Thad A. Brown says in his book on migration and politics, "While re-creating the experiences of migrants and their environments…it is useful to keep in mind the human drama of migration."[70]

Psychologists have sought to understand the complex behavioral components migrants face, at home and throughout their journey.

Mauricio Gaborit, PhD, is a social psychologist who studies the migration of children and adolescents at the Universidad Centroamericana José Simeón Cañas in El Salvador.

Mr. Gaborit conducted fifteen-minute interviews of children and teens deported from the United States to El Salvador, assessing for depression and anxiety. One of their most surprising findings was that deported children did not experience greater psychological harm than a control group of Salvadoran children who remained in the country.[71]

---

70 Thad A. Brown, *Migration and Politics: The Impact of Population Mobility on American Voting Behavior* (Chapel Hill, NC: The University of North Carolina Press, 2011).

71 Mauricio Gaborit, Mario Zetino Duarte, Carlos Iván Orellana, and Larissa Brioso, "Chapter 4. El Salvador," in *Childhood and Migration in Central and North America*, ed. Karen Musalo, Lisa Frydman, Pablo Ceriani Cernadas (Center for Gender and Refugee Studies, 2015).

As he puts it in a journal entry by the American Psychological Association, "To be a young person in El Salvador, Guatemala, or Honduras is extremely stressful...So stressful, in fact, that the migration route with all its perils barely registers above the daily pressures children and their families face here."[72]

This is not only the case among children. A study of 234 adults from El Salvador, Honduras, and Guatemala did a psychological assessment of trauma, depression, and other disorders among migrants seeking help in McAllen, Texas. According to the study, 32 percent of the sample met diagnostic criteria for PTSD, 24 percent for depression, and 17 percent for both disorders. Although this is just one study of a small sample, it indicates that a substantial number of these migrants have significant mental health symptoms.[73]

This data provides a stark contrast to the description of Central American immigrants contained in many media reports and political debates, as migrants motivated primarily by economic incentives. Structured interviews revealed high rates of trauma exposure, often including murdered family members, sexual and physical assault, death threats, extortion, and kidnapping. Very few participants reported that notifying the authorities resulted in an improvement to their situation, though most respondents acknowledged that they did not even try to seek assistance for fear of retaliation.

---

72 Mauricio Gaborit, Mario Zetino Duarte, Carlos Iván Orellana, and Larissa Brioso, "Chapter 4. El Salvador."

73 "Support for Central Americans," Monitor on Psychology (American Psychological Association, 2019).

Although much more research is needed to understand those psychological factors that push people to make the decision to leave, the fact that so many people (thousands in the case of the first caravan) are doing so is very telling of the conditions back home. From a behavioral perspective, the hardships are significant enough for some people that the struggles they may face when doing the trip up north is insignificant compared to what they might have been experiencing at home.

This leads us to try to unravel another important question: *What is it that these migrants were experiencing back home?*

The concept of a broken Central America is real. There is gang violence, high homicide rates, lack of economic opportunities, and many more structural problems, as we will see throughout the book. However, these characteristics, often cited as the culprits for pushing individuals away from these countries, are linked in an intricate way: they are all symptoms of a failing state, a state unable to provide protection and basic services to its citizens.

CHAPTER 6

THE ALLURE OF LEAVING

———

I met Patricia when I was only a baby. My parents had just arrived in Honduras and knew nobody, much like many other migrants when they arrive at a new destination. They needed someone to take care of me when they were busy, and they had no family nearby to help. When they met Patricia, their childcare problems were solved. Just like that, Patricia became our family in Honduras, and Honduras began to feel like home

Today, despite having a stable job and raising a beautiful and intelligent daughter in Honduras, she acknowledges that the allure of leaving to another country is real.

She and I have both agreed that in Central America, many of us have experienced an almost hypnotic admiration for the United States. The United States has, for a long time, been a sponsor to Central American countries (whether in a good way or a bad way is up to debate, but a sponsor nonetheless).

Many Central American countries have imported aspects of the American culture, such as fast food chains like

McDonalds, KFC, Burger King, Chili's, TGI Fridays, Ruby Tuesday, and Dunkin' Donuts. In addition, the availability of cable television from US sources, including CNN, Fox News, Cartoon Network, Nickelodeon, and many other channels, paired with the size of migrants moving from Central America to the United States has dramatically increased the adoption of North American ideas and values.[74]

For many years, I admired the United States for how wonderful, strong, and resilient a country it was.

In an almost subliminal and very subtle fashion, this cultural "fetishizing" of what the United States represents seeped into many individuals' image of what the American Dream meant.

Chris Valdes lived in Honduras for two years while he was directing a documentary in a town called Olancho. Chris, as I call him, lived in a street in the outskirts of town that had a couple of shops, the type of shops made with wooden plastic and maybe a sheet of metal here or there. One of these shops was a bike and car repair shop, where people could go in to solve their bike issues. That's when Chris met José.

"I became well acquainted with José over the course of the two years that I was there. He was about my age at the time: twenty-five years old. And he had a heart of gold. What was interesting about José was that during the two years that I knew him, he was saving up money."

---

74   Anne R. Pebley and Luis Rosero-Bixby, "Demographic Diversity and Change in the Central American Isthmus," (*Rand Corporation,* 1997)

"What for?" I asked quizzically.

"He was saving to pay a coyote to cross over to the US, not because he felt threatened, not because he wanted to make money, but because he really liked US's bike culture."

"Wait, what!" I was a little perplexed, but as someone who had lived in Honduras and had witnessed the awe many Hondurans and other Central Americans felt towards the United States, I realized that this was not the most outrageous thing out there.

"He had seen it in shows and movies. Through this, he had grown very fond of the bike culture: he liked fixing bikes, he liked to have his own bikes, and he felt like in Honduras, this culture did not exist. That's the main reason he wanted to go."

"And did he?" I asked immediately.

"That's the sad part," said Chris, pausing a little. "He was robbed. They took all of his money and tools. When he told me, I wanted to cry. I asked him what he was gonna do. He's religious, so he said that this was God's way of saying it wasn't the right time, and that whoever took the money probably needed it more than he did."

Living in Honduras, you hear stories again and again of people who were desperate to pursue a different life in the United States, who are convinced that moving is the best option, regardless of why it is.

In a way, there is an allure that draws people to the American dream, linked to the idea of a country that has historically valued its rule of law, has aimed to promote democracy, and has propagated this idea that if you work hard enough, you will make it. Even though, in today's age, the American Dream is harder to achieve than ever.

To someone living in a country with few opportunities, with many structural issues, and without any access to basic needs and services, the message of a different life can seem appealing.

Years ago, in a peanut factory in Honduras, a young man fell in love with a fifteen-year-old girl at work. Shortly after they began to spend time together, the young girl delivered him some life-changing news: she was pregnant. That day, he began to envision the life he and this fifteen-year-old girl could pursue in another country with their baby. He asked her to "cross the pond," as people colloquially say in Honduras, to migrate to the United States. "Are you staying or leaving?" he asked the girl. The girl's first reaction was positive: of course she would go. She too had dreams of having a family elsewhere. However, the more people she told about her plans, the more warnings she got on the dangers of travelling to the US. Eventually, she decided against it. His mind, however, was set on leaving, even if meant not seeing his baby.

That fifteen-year-old girl was Patricia, who was like my second mother while I lived in Honduras. She ended up staying in Honduras and raising her daughter, who today is studying to become a lawyer. By staying, she ended up helping my parents raise me as well.

However, had she left, she would have faced several obstacles, the ones her former partner and father of her daughter faced when he left all by himself.

On his first journey, he was almost was run over by a train.

Patricia's ex-partner is not the only person who faced a life or death experience as a result of having to ride the train. The death train, or "El tren de la muerte," is actually a freight train that often carries goods, like corn, cement, minerals. For migrants trying to get up north, "riding" the trains means sitting on top of cars, or between them.[75] Whenever there is a hard stop, the travelers take advantage of the moment to climb on or off.

On that trip, when Patricia's former partner was almost killed by that dangerous train, he was caught by border patrol and returned back home. Despite that, he did not give up. He tried a second time. And then on his third attempt, he finally made it past the border.

His deep belief that life was better elsewhere prompted him to try to move to the United States not just once, but three times, even if it meant not seeing his baby again or dying.

Patricia's neighbor also went on the journey and was not as lucky. The train destroyed half of his leg. Even this was a rosy outcome, as Patricia said that had he not jumped off at

---

75   Joseph Sorrentino, "Train of the Unknowns: Crossing the Border Isn't as Hard as Getting To It." (*Commonweal,* November 2012).

the right time, his whole body would have succumbed to the train's weight, ending his life.

As Patricia recalled, when she was at the verge of leaving for the United States, she commented on her life in Honduras today.

"I am happy in Honduras because I have a daughter and I have built my life here. But that does not compensate for how difficult it is to live here, especially if you are not one of the rich families. People know that things can be better elsewhere. I had a friend called Maria who left to Spain years ago, and continued telling all of her friends how much happier she was there. She even tried to convince me to join her, again and again. Who knows how true it is whether another country is better than your own. But in the moment, it all seems worth it, like a fresh new start."

I told Patricia I was thankful she did not move off to Spain with her friend Maria. That I loved being with her during my time in Honduras, and that I appreciated her for taking care of me for many years. And yet, deep down, I know firsthand some of the struggles Patricia has faced. Struggles that could have pushed her to take that decision.

For Patricia to get to my house, she took several buses and walked several blocks. For months, a man continuously targeted her on her way to my house, a robber who carried a gun to intimidate women and steal their money, jewelry, or whatever he could snatch. She avoided the streets where he usually lurked but stumbling upon him was sometimes inevitable.

More than once she came into the house in the morning, panicking. Shaking. Telling me that she had just had a gun pointed at her head. As a young fifteen-year-old or so, I wondered why she hadn't reported it to the cops. Patricia explained it very concisely: "They will do nothing. This would not be the first time a woman reported the incident, without any action whatsoever. There's no point in trying."

One time, he stole (among other things) the key to our house. My family had given Patricia a key so she could get in and out as she pleased. After that incident, she, by her own will, decided she would never carry the key around ever again. That she would rather ring the doorbell and wait a little for us to open the door than risk our safety.

The robber only stopped terrorizing her after justice was served. The guard that protected a wealthy family's house realized that he was bothering women close to their street. The guard killed him. I guess that was more efficient than waiting for the justice system to convict him for all the women he had targeted.

We changed the lock to our house. However, even after the guy was killed and the lock changed, I occasionally had dreams in which the house's walls were melting in the middle of the night and a group of bandits made their way in. Even before the incident, I grew up concocting ways to escape my house by creating a bridge between my window that connected to the roof and my neighbor's roof. Just in case.

It wasn't far-fetched—I had heard too many stories. Not long before Patricia's key was stolen, some people had broken into our neighbors' house and had roped them to a chair, taking everything. My neighbors escaped unharmed, but for me, it caused a great deal of anxiety. Incidents like this one occurred frequently in Honduras, so much that our society had almost normalized them. But there was nothing normal about something so terrifying happening so close to our home.

What if we were next?

A couple of years before that, my brother's classmate had been kidnapped from his own room and returned only after he paid a ransom. His family left the country immediately.

The most tragic of all was a neighbor of ours—someone who had just been in my house drinking wine with my parents a month prior—who was kidnapped close to his house and later killed. His family also left immediately. These were just people I knew—it was not uncommon to hear stories of other victims.

Through the years, I had developed a habit of looking behind me while our garage door was closing to check that nobody was walking in. To me, it seemed like the best way to raid a house. Our next-door neighbors, also very close to my family, had their own protective measures. They owned multiple guns in case they were ever targeted.

When I moved to the United States, I couldn't understand how people in the apartments or town houses in Georgetown could ever forget or neglect to close their front door. Any time we got an email posting about a home burglary, it was because someone left their door open. It always made me chuckle. It was such a rookie mistake.

What is the allure of leaving? People might face challenges along the way, like the death train. And adapting can be harder than expected.

To some people, like Patricia, the allure of leaving is only a temptation, a thought that hasn't concretized but that lingers in the background. To others, like her former partner who tried to enter the US three times, the allure of a life elsewhere makes the sacrifice and struggles associated with moving worth it. The question is: why is the allure so strong, and why has it been that way for such a long time? What are people living with at home that makes leaving the best option?

In the next section, I go deeper into some of the systemic issues that make it so difficult to live in Central America: how the conditions in these countries affect people's livelihoods; how the states have, due to how weak they are, become unable to protect individuals in their home countries; how the local conditions are an important reason why people's lives in Central America can be hard.

CHAPTER 7

SUB-STATES

———

Chris Valdes and his colleague attended a local gathering in the rural municipality of Bocas del Monte, Olancho. In this town where everyone knew each other, they were outsiders. In fact, Chris and his colleague were the only North Americans to visit Bocas del Monte for as long as anyone in the village could recall. Upon entering, he couldn't help but notice people staring or whispering under their breath as they walked through. He didn't care that he stuck out to most people—until the host of the gathering noticed them. The host was a powerful local politician and business magnate.

He was also a drug lord.

Chris saw the drug lord sitting on top of a pickup truck, large gun next to him, handing out beers. Chris avoided making eye contact with him and heeded the locals' cautionary advice to avoid drawing attention to himself. But the drug lord knew everyone, except him and his colleague. And that bothered him.

The drug lord's eyes pierced Chris, and he swiftly stood up.

Oh shoot, thought Chris. He hoped it was nothing.

But the drug lord took another step.

And another.

And another.

All in Chris' direction.

Finally, the drug lord stood in front of Chris, with a gun in hand and a grimace on his face.

"He interrogated us and asked what we were doing. It was clear from his tone and aggressive body language that he didn't trust us. Meanwhile, all I did was eyeball the gun he still held in his hand. A huge gun."

The drug lord asked about a person named Balbino, who happened to be Chris' friend's father.

This was a million-dollar question. Maybe the drug lord hated Balbino and if Chris said yes, he and his colleague were dead.

"Yes," Chris said.

His heart pumped as he awaited the drug lord's response. He walked the tightrope of life and death.

"Balbino is...practically my brother!" They passed the test. But things could have gone differently. The informal leaders of this community were willing to do anything to protect their territory. Even if it meant killing.

Max Weber's classical theory of statehood portrays a state's main characteristic as a territory claiming the monopoly of the legitimate use of physical force to enforce and maintain order.[76]

For Weber, the legitimate use of force is measured in terms of the state's fiscal and legal capacity. Fiscal capacity entails the state's ability to tax in order to provide public goods. In terms of legal capacity, he identifies the state's supremacy as sole arbiter of conflict resolution and contract enforcement.

But what happens when Max Weber's theory applies to sub-regions, areas where gang members, or drug lords, have more authority than the government? What happens when government institutions are unable to penetrate its thick symbolic border? Chris' experience in Olancho shaped his opinion on what it means to live within those symbolic borders.

"I feel like in Honduras there is a sense that, because there is a lack of central power or authority, you have other players come in and fill that void. Those players can sometimes be the police, in a corrupt way, or families, or narcos. And especially in Olancho, it has formed an almost autonomous sentiment where people feel empowered...like they are on their own. It kind of reminds me of how the United States

---

76 Max Weber. Politics as a Vocation. *From Max Weber: Essays in Sociology*, (2014):89-140.

would have been in the early eighteenth century when people were moving out West and had to fend for themselves."

He also pointed out that Olancho operates so independently and autonomously within its territory that the first case of coronavirus only started in late May, whereas in the capital city and other parts of the country it had started in mid- and late-March. Why? Because they set up a militia at the border that was not letting anyone come or go, with the exception of certain essential people. They physically created a sub-state to protect the inside.

In Honduras, powerful actors who use tight measures to protect their territory are common. As a member of a Costa Rican women's organization, my mother planned fundraising events to benefit people living in a remote town of Honduras. However, a gang controlled the town and only allowed one person to enter in and out of the community: Friar Jorge. He was a church member who had built a bond of trust with the gang members for years. Everyone else had to keep out.

In Bocas del Monte, Olancho, the drug lord also fended for the people, providing what the government had failed to: money and protection. He was like the godfather.

The drug cartel protected and sponsored people like Manuel, the main protagonist in Chris' documentary, *Olancho*.[77] Manuel is a band member who wrote and performed songs praising a drug cartel in Olancho, and in return was paid a

---

77 Christopher Valdes and Theodore Grisold, *Olancho* (2017) documentary.

substantial amount of money by the cartel. These songs are what have come to be called *narco-corridas*.

For Manuel and his band, the risk was worth it because it paid well and was prestigious. The band members that Chris spoke to all came from families that had historically been subsistence farmers in Boca del Monte, Olancho. For a day of working the fields and selling coffee and corn, they earned five dollars. When they played music for the cartels, they made $250 to $400 a night, approximately forty times more.

On top of the extra income that singing and working for the cartels generated, the band members became local celebrities. By singing for the drug lords, Manuel and his band gained popularity and recognition in Olancho. "He would get free meals in restaurants as a sign of admiration. People recognized him everywhere in that territory."

But more than anything, Chris pointed out that they somehow felt protected by the cartel they served. And they felt powerful.

However, Manuel was taking a risk: peripherally engaging in the drug trade. They were not doing anything illegal, but their sponsor was. This same fame they garnered through music was a curse in disguise. One of the songs became so popular it was played in the local radio. That's how members of the rival cartel first heard the song, and they were not happy. They wanted blood. Manuel knew he was in trouble.

In this situation, Manuel was unprotected by the cartel who had backed him up during his days of fame. The state, on the other hand, had never fended for him. He migrated to North Carolina, fleeing the persecution he was experiencing at home.

The presence of stronger actors trying to fill the power void is an indication of state fragility, a condition that pushes people like Manuel, to flee. According to a report by the Inter-American Dialogue, migration has grown since 2010 and is directly associated with political fragility and instability in eight countries in the Latin American region: Colombia, Cuba, El Salvador, Guatemala, Haiti, Honduras, Nicaragua, and Venezuela. Half of the list are Central American countries.[78]

The sad reality is that these territories, although officially under the rule of governments, are subdued by groups so powerful that they are capable of thwarting the country's legal system in their favor. Even police officers are scared of these groups, and rightfully so.

When I was seventeen years old, I met a guy who I became very fond of. He was also the son of the head of the police in Tegucigalpa. We had many friends in common, so I quickly became acquainted with him and his group, seeing him at house parties and social events. One weekend, I took a picture with him and three other friends and posted it on Instagram. Years later, while scrolling through my Instagram, I saw that picture of him and shuddered. I deleted it immediately.

---

78 Manuel Orozco. "Latin America and the Caribbean Migration from Weak and Failing States." *Inter-American Dialogue*, (July 2019): 5-6

Because a couple of weeks after we had taken that picture and I posted it on Instagram, something tragic happened. He had been killed while eating at a restaurant—a revenge attack against his father.

I think that is why the police fear these actors, because of this level of retaliation.

On other occasions, the police are the problem, abusing their power.

Magaly is from Nicaragua, but now she lives in Costa Rica. She had a terrible childhood because of her abusive mother. "One day I hunted a deer, and then my mother and her husband, my stepdad, ate the entire deer together and only let me eat one tortilla with salt. That's how it always was. I did most of the work, and she took everything for herself." Because her mother made her work so hard, Magaly never went to school. And she never learned how to read.

Her mother never defended her—even when her perverted stepdad watched Magaly showering naked. Whenever Magaly complained to her mother, she would respond with beatings that sometimes left her bleeding. She still has scars on her back from these episodes. Magaly hated her mother and her stepdad. One time, Magaly tried to stab her stepdad, but he dodged the knife.

Magaly was only approximately fifteen years old when her own mother made her have intercourse with Noel, just because he bought them coffee, food, and "stupid presents," as Magaly explained. In a very poor home, where there is essentially no income, her mother reckoned she would at least use her daughter to her advantage. "He was disgusting to me. He was seventeen years older. I wanted to kiss the boys my age. I wasn't ready for this."

Her mother would even set up the bed in their own house for him to spend the night with Magaly. Magaly was particularly concerned that she would end up pregnant, so she got access to contraceptive pills. Unfortunately, Noel found out and got so angry that he threatened to hurt her if she didn't stop. She ended up pregnant.

"I feel terrible saying this, but it is the truth. After I found out I was pregnant, I would make my younger brother and my nephew jump on top of my stomach: just bounce, bounce, bounce. I was trying to have an abortion. Then I climbed a tree that I was going to jump off from. But Noel, the baby's father, saw me climb the tree and knew what I was up to. He grabbed his gun from his pocket and started shooting at the air."

I asked Magaly: "Did you ever try to tell the cops what was going on in your household? About Noel?"

"Oh…Noel was actually a police officer."

When she told me that, it took me a while for it to sink in. To realize that this whole time, part of the hell in her life was propagated by someone who was meant to protect her. It unveiled the incredibly thwarted system she lived in.

There are several definitions of what constitutes a fragile state, but there is general consensus that it has characteristics that impair their economic and social performance: weak governance, limited administrative capacity, chronic humanitarian crises, persistent social tensions, and often violence or the legacy of armed conflict and civil war.

All these characteristics lead to a state unable to protect its citizens. This same dynamic puts people who are not sponsored by powerful groups at greater risk of abuse and exploitation. It is in this circumstance that migration becomes a feasible option.

As Manuel Orozco, Director at the Center for Migration and Economic Stabilization at Creatives Associate International puts it, "These countries exhibit major political challenges which in most cases approach state failure or poor rule of law. There is a negative relationship between the growth in migration in the region and state governance (a measure of fragility). As performance in governance deteriorates, migration growth increases from those countries that are most affected by state fragility. Migrants from these fragile states amount to nearly thirteen million people, or nearly 40 percent of all Latin American migration of any kind."[79]

---

79   Orozco. 6-7

CHAPTER 8

THE DEATH OF ENTREPRENEURSHIP

———

Patricia, who took care of me growing up, is an incredible cook. She can prepare anything, from mouthwatering handmade Honduran corn tortillas to delicious grilled steak with a homemade sauce that is to die for to fresh Italian pasta and pesto made from scratch. She also has that rare talent of preparing the most heart-warming, homey, and delicious meal with whatever scraps of food are available. It is like magic. I often joked with Patricia, asking why she didn't open her own restaurant.

She used to laugh it off. It was fear, she said, that kept her from opening a restaurant, and not merely the fear of failure. Patricia was terrified she might fall into the deadly trap she'd seen others encounter in a country where criminal organizations control enterprise and force entrepreneurs to pay the *impuesto de guerro*, or war tax.

"Here you cannot even put up a gum stand without being charged the impuesto de guerra," she explained. "You see those women who are making tortillas in the middle of the street? Even they have to pay! Not too long ago a school closed down as well because it was being extorted. It is outrageous how much money criminal organizations and gangs make."

Patricia told me about her friend Josefina, who lived in Comayagüela, Honduras, and who had opened a small baleada restaurant. Baleada is a delicious typical Honduran food consisting of a thick flour tortilla filled with refried beans and a variety of other foods: avocado, cheese, plantain, and more, depending on the person's preference. For homesick Hondurans living elsewhere, this is one of the first local meals they miss.

Josefina's stand was the place to be, with frequent customers purchasing baleadas for lunch on a regular basis. Soon enough, her reputation spread like wildfire. Long lines would form every day, and her stand was always full to the brim.

She received the war tax. Josefina closed down her baleada place and is currently gaging what to do next. Patricia highlights that Josefina was lucky her extortioners were gracious enough to not kill her; they only stole some things from her stand. That's minor damage.

Josefina does not have an income anymore because her business was forcibly shut down. She cannot get help from the government because the government of Honduras does not have unemployment protection or support.

Patricia's fear of suffering Josefina's same fate halted her from becoming an entrepreneur.

Organized crime continues to control the lives of business owners and workers in Honduras. *InSight Crime* classifies the region as an extortion hotspot: in 2015, Salvadorans paid an estimated four hundred million dollars annually in extortion fees, followed by Hondurans, who paid an estimated two hundred million dollars, and Guatemalans, who paid an estimated sixty-one million dollars. The report warns that despite these shocking numbers, the actual figures may be higher, given that extortion is one of the most underreported crimes.[80]

One of the most affected sectors is public transportation. According to *InSight Crime*, buses and taxis pay an estimated twenty-five million dollars in Honduras, and thirty-four million dollars in El Salvador in extortions per year.[81]

As a group that is highly targeted by criminal organizations, workers are literally risking their lives as they work. In the same report, *InSight Crime* writes that over three hundred workers in the Honduran transportation sector were killed between 2011 and 2015, and more than thirty-six Salvadoran transportation workers were killed in 2015 alone. In Guatemala, between 2007 and 2015, over five hundred bus drivers were killed in violent incidents.[82]

---

80 Dudley, Steven and Michael Lohmuller, "Northern Triangle is World's Extortion Hotpost," *InSight Crime,* July 2015.

81 Dudley, Steven, "InSide: The Most Dangerous Job in the World," *InSight Crime,* March 2011.

82 Dudley and Lohmuller. "Northern Triangle is World's Extortion Hotpost."

For Patricia, those numbers hit too close to home. Her brother drives a bus, and because of a recent incident, she worries for his safety. Her friend's family member who worked as a bus driver was killed by a gang that was extorting him.

"I pray to God every day that he doesn't get a letter requesting the impuesto de guerra."

The *impuesto de guerra* is not only a form of extortion; it is a boundary to self-driven individuals who are trying to make a living and have an income. It keeps people like Josefina down, who had started their own micro business just to have them crushed in a second.

To those who have never started a business, there is an immediate disincentive to ever open a business at all. To those who do own a business, there is a constant fear that they will have to succumb to a criminal organization or gang's whims. In this context, any person with even a hint of entrepreneurial spirit is quickly discouraged.

The presence of the *impuesto de guerra* is one of the categories of violence that leads to out-migration. In 2015, Doctors Without Borders (MSF) carried out a survey of 467 randomly sampled migrants and refugees coming from Honduras, El Salvador, and Guatemala. Almost 40 percent of respondents mentioned direct attacks or threats to themselves or their families, extortion or gang-forced recruitment as the main reason for fleeing their countries. Specifically looking at extortion, 54.8 percent of the Salvadorans had been the victim of blackmail or extortion.[83]

I spoke to another Honduran woman, named Laura, who also suffered due to gang extortion. One day, Laura was sitting down waiting for customers in her store, a small *pulperia* (convenience store) that she ran herself in a Honduran neighborhood called Loarque. She had recently opened her own business, one that, albeit small, would help provide for her baby boy. She was a single mother, and having her own business provided her flexibility and enough income to sustain them both. Little did she know, her decision to open this business would backfire and would force a large gap between her and her only son.

Before she even opened that store, Laura had really tried to make a living in Honduras. She switched jobs several times, always doing her best to make ends meet.

She used to work at Pizza Hut in Toncontin, the airport at Tegucigalpa. But after she got pregnant, she quit to take care of the baby. However, when the expenses started catching up, she found herself in desperate need for a job. After searching everywhere, she began working at a sewing shop, where she spent four years working. Then she switched to a job working at a Chinese restaurant where she was employed for twelve years.

Then she was fired.

---

83 "Forced to Flee Central America's Northern Triangle: A Neglected Humanitarian Crisis," *Médecins Sans Frontières,* May 2017: 5.

That's when she opened the pulpería. During that critical juncture of her life, it seemed like the best option for her and her son. Then everything changed that day in her store when she saw a group of men walk in. They were gang members.

"The day these gang members walked into the pulpería the first time, a Sunday afternoon, I was terrified. The guy came in and said that he was coming back on Thursday, and that he wanted a set amount of money. That if I didn't pay that money, I would die. I had no doubt in my mind that he meant it."

Laura had heard about the infamous war tax many times, read about it in the news, heard her friends talk about how they had been affected. But as a mother trying to make a living, she had crossed her fingers that she would be overlooked by the gang members.

Laura was particularly nervous because of recent news. That same gang group that was threatening her with extortion had been responsible for a recent killing in her same neighborhood: a duel between that gang and another gang. "In the process of seeking revenge, there were casualties. They even killed a kid and dog in the process."

As she told me her story, Laura excused herself for a second as she fought back the tears while remembering her son, who still lives in Honduras. "Se me hace un nudo en la garganta... my throat is a tight knot." The fact that she had been forcefully separated from her son, after having started her own business with the hopes of being a better provider for him, is a painful realization that crosses my mind.

I told Laura that we don't have to continue talking about it if doesn't feel comfortable doing so. "No, I want this story to be heard because this continues happening in Honduras. I am one of many, and it needs to stop."

Laura had a cousin living in Costa Rica, so she decided to move there. She left two years ago, in May.

A state, to paraphrase Weber, is an administrative region with the legitimate use of force that allows that specific region to tax. Isn't this what these criminal organizations and gangs are doing? Although in English it is called extortion, in Central American countries it is called a war tax, precisely because it works like a tax. It is money collected by an entity that is powerful enough to coerce people into voluntarily (although under threatening circumstances) contributing part of their income.

As an economist for a non-partisan NGO, Alejandro Kafatti monitors the budget and execution of resources in the Honduran government entities. I asked him whether the government has taken actions to address the issue of extortions.

"The government will tell you that it has its policies to contain extortion. A multi-disciplinary force was created between the police and the military called the National Anti-Extortion Force and the National Anti-Maras and Gang Force that work together with resources from the Ministry of Security and the Ministry of Defense. However, we are seeing that it is a reactive response to the problems, that is, from a time when extortion had reached such a high extent that the government had to invest more resources in arms, ammunition, and security forces in order to contain it. However, from a budgetary perspective, there has been no spending on preventive measures at all."

I will confess that if I was in the government and given the task to stop extortion and, more broadly speaking, gang violence, I would probably start crying. I can truly empathize with the difficult position leaders in Central American countries go through in the face of this phenomena that only continues to spread and spread, like a disease. How difficult it must be to stop gangs from extorting citizens and to stop gangs altogether—period.

However, there is one thing I cannot empathize with, a phenomenon that we know all too well in the Central American region. While gangs are draining individuals' resources by requesting the war tax, the state is requesting taxes as well. Unfortunately, this tax money is sometimes mismanaged, going down the drain.

CHAPTER 9

WHAT RESILIENCE REALLY LOOKS LIKE

———

A father came into his young son's room, the night before leaving for the United States. He had lined up a job, and although the opportunity would help him provide for his eleven children and wife, the thought of being far away from them pained him. The door creaked as the father stepped in and crouched next to his sleeping son. He began sobbing and saying, "Mi hijito, mi hijito," my son, my son.

Carlos is among my dearest friends in Costa Rica, so when he tells this story, I can't help but empathize.

Every time Carlos tells this story, I picture his parents' small house in Costa Rica. I imagine his father sneaking into Carlos' boyhood bedroom, unaware that the sound of the creaking door had awakened him from his sleep. I imagine Carlos pretending to be asleep, then suddenly paralyzed by intense emotion as he hears his father sobbing. I picture Carlos realizing this was goodbye, but not wanting it to be.

Carlos' father flew out the next day. But when he reached immigration control in the United States, he encountered a problem: having eleven children at home raised a red flag. The officer immediately returned him to Costa Rica.

Carlos didn't care. He was beyond grateful that his father would be around. But for a poor and struggling family, this meant that everyone had to contribute and help out at home. To generate extra income for the household, Carlos' mother used to prepare baked goods and would send him and his siblings to sell them in the streets.

Despite growing up in a low-resource home, Carlos received a good public education. Characterized by his discipline, he spent endless hours studying.

Costa Rica's most prestigious public university granted him acceptance to study law. Because Carlos could not pay for it, he worked for the university and earned a stipend that paid for his studies and for additional expenses. He never held any debt, thanks to the university's support.

Today, Carlos is a successful lawyer. However, he could never have done it without the opportunities he had at home: a quality public education with options available for people coming from a low-resource background.

Carlos accomplished something that many people in other countries cannot achieve due to lack of quality education or job opportunities. Like Carlos' father, many breadwinners look for opportunities elsewhere. This was the case with Jorge.

In 2001, during a typical January day, Jorge left the place he had called home for many years: Nicaragua. He arrived in San José, Costa Rica, on a chilly Sunday night at 9 p.m. with only fifty dollars in his pocket and a dream to support his wife and kids.

A forty-three-year-old man, Jorge had worked in a company dedicated to exporting non-traditional goods, such as *pitaya* (a traditional Nicaraguan fruit), ginger, and other crops. He knew that staying in Nicaragua meant having the same job forever, with no opportunity to grow.

"At least back then, when I left, it wasn't the same to go to college in Nicaragua as going to college in Costa Rica. Also, it was so common to work, work, work without even making ends meet. Working brutal hours merely to survive."

Right before leaving, Jorge told his wife, "Don't worry about me! Once I find a job, everything will be good. I will be able to provide for our family."

Jorge began working in a crop export company in the town of Siquirres. His relentless dedication to his job payed off years later, as he went from being a peon to earning a chief position for three divisions within the company.

Despite Jorge's success, he faced challenges while living in Costa Rica. For the next years, he would live far away from his family. Technology was not advanced enough to bridge the distance gap, and he often felt lonely.

Two years after arriving in Siquirres, he had a motorcycle accident. He broke his tibia, clavicle, and calf bone, forcing him to wear a cast for nine months. The accident immobilized him, a terrible setback for someone attempting to thrive in a job that required full body mobility. Jorge could not even go to the bathroom or shower by himself while recovering from the accident, which was especially embarrassing for him.

"But God never abandons you," Jorge said. "He always places angels along the way."

Jorge's friend Heiner welcomed him in his home and took care of him. As they spent many hours together, Jorge grew a deep connection with Heiner, to the extent that Heiner felt like a brother to him.

They spent so much time together that Jorge started helping Heiner do his job, preparing estimations and projections for their client and one of the world's largest produce supplier, Del Monte Foods Inc. Little by little, Jorge became incredibly skilled at doing Heiner's job.

Jorge recovered, and everything seemed to go back to normal. But two months later, another tragedy struck. One night, while leaving a party in Herediana, a burglar shot Heiner in the ribs. He lost a lot of blood, but his situation would soon grow even more devastating.

When Jorge returned to work the next Monday morning, company management requested that he finish Heiner's projections to meet the usual deadline for their clients. Rumor had spread that Heiner had taught him these valuable skills. It was a golden opportunity, so Jorge agreed. While Heiner fought for his life, Jorge covered for him at work.

Soon after Jorge turned in his assignment, the general manager approached him with a congratulatory tone: "You have earned this position. From now you will be the Chief of Estimations." This seemed like too great a responsibility for someone who had been working in the field. It certainly made him nervous. "Back then, we exported forty thousand boxes of pineapple a week to Europe and the United States. It was a big deal." He quickly accepted the position.

Jorge did not realize that by assuming this role, he would betray his friend. "Now that you are Chief of Estimations, you have a new duty," the general manager told Jorge as he placed an envelope in his hands. Jorge glanced at it. Confusion became agitation as he realized it was a termination letter addressed to Heiner.

For some time, management had not been happy with Heiner's performance, and his habit of partying. This was a good opportunity to get rid of him. Jorge felt remorse as he approached Heiner's house to deliver the news. He felt guilty for what he was about to do. After delivering the news, he felt even worse, as Heiner simply said, "Don't worry about it. It's okay, I'll figure it out."

Things soon changed for Jorge. He received a higher salary, was gifted a truck, and received two promotions.

He feels a deep sense of gratitude for his company and Costa Rica. However, he never thought that by moving he would face so many obstacles. "I never thought I would face such difficult situations, like breaking my bones while being alone and having to fire my friend."

I asked him what would have happened if he had stayed in Nicaragua.

"Thank God I left. When I think of Nicaragua, I feel conflicted. But even my wife, who years later joined me in Costa Rica and has pressured me to go back, knows the opportunities here are better for us. Nicaragua's economy is volatile because of the social and political unrest, and we don't want to be part of it."

Jorge is not wrong. Due to the unrest in the country since April of 2018, the economy contracted by 4.0 and 3.9 percent in 2018 and 2019 respectively. For 2020, growth is expected to fall by 6.3 percent as a result of COVID-19 and continued political and social unrest.[84]

People living in other countries have also worked hard to make a living in other destinations. In Chapter 1, I introduced you to Guillermo, a student and taxi driver who fled El Salvador with his family during a period of civil war and started a new life in New York.

---

84 "The World Bank in Nicaragua," *The World Bank*, Web, accessed September 25, 2020.

"At first, we lived with my parents in a small studio, my pregnant wife, my boy, and my parents," Guillermo recalled. "During that time, my wife was bursting with our second child, and I quickly looked for a job for extra income. I found a job at a Marshall's store, in the delivery section. I organized clothes by price, types of garment, etc. During that time, cassette tapes were popular, and while I was working at Marshall's, I would listen to tapes to learn English vocabulary. I barely spoke English, but the cassettes helped me learn."

Guillermo confessed he worked in every job he could take.

"I'm not embarrassed of it. I have done everything to support my family. I have been the newspaper boy, passing through neighborhoods at 6 a.m. every morning. When I finished two hours later, I would go to my next job. Then I found a job as driver for a school bus."

After having lived in New York for five years, he decided it was time to leave.

"We lived near a town called Garden City. Although Garden City was a rich neighborhood, two blocks away, there was a city called Hempstead in Long Island; that's where we lived. I wasn't very happy in the neighborhood because the area was crowded, very dirty, and sometimes dangerous."

His brother had recently moved to Maryland, and after one visit, Guillermo realized the area was less crowded and cleaner than New York. Maryland was ideal for his quickly growing family.

"By then I had three kids already. I left for a month to find a job and then brought the rest of the family with me. My brother had gotten a job painting cars, so he taught me how to paint cars too. That's how I started working for a dealer."

He faced many challenges. "Even though I was happy to have a job that paid well, I learned that my job was actually dangerous. One day I looked at the paint labels and realized they had a warning saying that the chemicals in the paint could kill you. I used to wear a protective mask, but I always thought that one day I was going to lose a lung. I decided I needed to find another job."

Guillermo completely changed careers. "I told myself that I could also sell homes, that I could do it. So, I signed up to the Real Estate Courses. My boss at the dealer was upset. He said, 'Why are you leaving us? You are making good money here!' All I said was, this is good money, but it will kill me! I told him the truth, that I have a large family and they need me to be alive for a while!"

The day Guillermo went to his first realtor class and introduced himself to his new classmates, he realized he was an exception in the group. Everyone either had a college degree, knew about finances, or had worked as bank tellers. And then there was Guillermo. "When they asked me what I did, I said I was a car painter. They couldn't believe it!"

And yet, he completed the classes and became a successful realtor for many years. After the 2008 crash in the housing market, Guillermo teamed up with a dentist friend, and ran the business side of a dentistry office. He and his partner offered accessible prices. "Back then, a denture usually was around fifteen hundred dollars. We would do them for five to six hundred dollars. Because of our low prices, the volume of patients grew. It was a win-win; we had a large clientele, and we helped people, especially Hispanics, access affordable services."

Years after having left El Salvador, Guillermo constantly thinks of new ways to cease migration coming from his country by creating opportunities at home. For some time, he ran a chicken farm in his city in hopes that it would generate local jobs. Although he ran it while still living in the US, he was motivated with the ability to somehow help his country. He had to sell the farm, he said, when larger corporations undercut his prices and crushed his small business. But even that didn't crush his commitment to helping his country.

Despite the odds against him, Guillermo managed to support his family through hard work. If he had stayed home, he wouldn't be where he is today. Students graduating from his university in El Salvador only found jobs as professors with low salaries. In the United States, despite many challenges, he stayed afloat, bought a house by the time he had six kids, and raised a happy family.

In general, the region lacks economic opportunities and has widespread poverty. In a 2017 survey, 53 percent of Hondurans, 49 percent of Guatemalans, and 29 percent of Salvadorans lived on less than $5.50 a day.[85] Furthermore, the labor

---

85 Emmanuel Abuelafia, Giselle Del Carmen, Marta Ruiz-Arranz, "Tras los pasos del migrante: Perspectivas y experiencias de la migración de

market cannot absorb the one hundred thousand young people entering the labor force each year. In 2017, a quarter of young people in Honduras, Guatemala, and El Salvador were neither working nor studying, above the 21.4-percent average in Latin America and the Caribbean.[86] Not surprisingly, among the migrants who reported lack of economic opportunity as the main reason for migrating, 54 percent specified that this was due to unemployment.

Even those with a solid education cannot find a job.

As part of a documentary she was producing, Esther Anino followed a group of young Central Americans who attended a hip-hop dance contest called Reyes de Centroamérica. The event was part of an initiative to provide individuals in marginalized communities a space for artistic expression.

Esther interviewed several participants, but one person stuck out: a young Guatemalan.

"He had been looking for a job for four years. As we spoke, I noticed something: this man had great analytical capacity and excellent vocabulary. I realized that, very likely, his inability to find a job was not because he was not qualified. It was because in his community, there probably were no opportunities, period."

El Salvador, Guatemala y Honduras en Estados Unidos," *Inter-American Development Bank* (December 2019: 12).

86 Emmanuel Abuelafia, Giselle Del Carmen, Marta Ruiz-Arranz, "Tras los pasos del migrante: Perspectivas y experiencias de la migración de El Salvador, Guatemala y Honduras en Estados Unidos": 12.

Two weeks after Esther's conversation with him, and just two weeks before the COVID-19 lockdown, he migrated to the United States. Without ushering a single word to any of the colleagues or anyone else in the dance group.

Despite Esther's shock with his sudden decision, she saw it coming. "He kept emphasizing how he really could not find a job, how there were no economic opportunities. I don't know what happened to him after he left. I hope he made it before COVID-19 really hit the US. I just know he had potential."

Many people who leave are not necessarily people without an education. According to the IDB survey to Northern Triangle countries, seven out of ten migrants living in the United States have completed secondary education, a higher proportion that those individuals in the same age range living in their home country. However, this does not necessarily make them qualified in the United States. Compared to other migrants entering the country, their level and quality of education is still low.[87]

Whereas Carlos, my dear friend, was lucky enough to have excellent public education at home, other people don't have that privilege. Iran, a young Guatemalan man, shared Carlos' conviction that education was the answer, but migrated to Costa Rica to pursue it.

"In my high school years, I moved to a different part of Guatemala called Port in Izabala, in Santo Tomás de Castilla.

---

87   Emmanuel Abuelafia, Giselle Del Carmen, Marta Ruiz-Arranz, "Tras los pasos del migrante: Perspectivas y experiencias de la migración de El Salvador, Guatemala y Honduras en Estados Unidos": 9.

Although I made some friends and enjoyed the area, there was a problem. Once I graduated from a technical high school, my classmates and I were expected to start working immediately. It was embedded in the system because we were attending technical schools and nobody went to college. My high school concentration, for instance, was welding."

Iran had higher aspirations. At an early age, he dreamed of going to college and studying clinical engineering, a major that did not even exist in the university at Port in Izabala.

His plan was to study at the University of Costa Rica, the same school Carlos attended years ago, but he had no money to go. A year after graduating from high school, Iran's brother got five free cellphones at work, and he told Iran that if he was able to sell them, he could keep the money.

"I got $200 from selling the cellphones. I bought a one-way bus ride to Costa Rica, and I embarked on my journey."

During his first year in San José, he struggled to make a living. "There were some months that were harder, and I couldn't eat every meal. Usually I ate rice and beans because it was the cheapest." However, he found a place of community at a local church. Church members who heard his story supported him with food baskets or hired him to do small jobs. "Sometimes, I transferred music from cassettes to CDs. Other times, I cleaned their homes. At some point, I also worked at a gas station, and sold baked goods using my mother's recipes. Anything to make ends meet! I never said no!"

A year after arriving in San José, Iran took the University of Costa Rica entrance exam, an important step in determining whether he could gain acceptance into the university, and to a specific major. Medical school, for instance, requires the highest entrance score out of all the majors, while other majors require lower scores.

He failed the exam. His low score barred him from gaining access to all available majors, even those with the lowest entrance exam grade requirements. By expecting him to be a welder, the technical school he attended in Guatemala failed him too.

"But I didn't give up. With the money I had saved from selling goods and from other side jobs, I paid for classes to prepare me for the exam. I was able to gain entrance into the University of Costa Rica the following year, for the clinical engineering major."

Recently, Iran graduated. I asked him what he is up to these days, after achieving his dream of attending college.

"The past months have been chaotic because of COVID-19. I had been planning to open a cafe near the University of Costa Rica, because there are always young people there, many potential customers. I thought I was going to make a living that way. But then the lockdown burnt down this possibility."

I was sad to hear that this plan had failed. This was the first time I was speaking to Iran, and through his story and all his endeavors and resilience, I wanted him to succeed.

"But last week I got exciting news. I was accepted for an important position at the Coca-Cola Company in Costa Rica. As always, I am going to do the best I can and deliver the best results!"

I have no doubt in my mind that this is true.

Despite finishing college and obtaining a job, Iran faced obstacle after obstacle before achieving success. Coming from a home of immigrant parents from El Salvador, and living in a difficult neighborhood, Brenda also experienced challenges throughout her lifetime—challenges that dragged along with her into college.

The sound of police sirens startled Brenda and a group of middle school students as they smoked weed and drank near some train tracks. Brenda had done nothing wrong— she didn't drink, and she certainly didn't smoke. But the fear that the police would associate her with the rest of the clique ushered her to sprint away even more quickly. Amid her hopelessness, her neighbors found a back alleyway that led them directly home. She was safe, but guilt bubbled up as her mother's voice warning her to steer away from drugs, alcohol, and vices replayed in her head. She never wanted to find herself in that situation ever again.

Minutes prior, Brenda had awkwardly sat on the floor and attempted to read her book as two of her neighbors, also seventh graders, had dragged her along to participate in their clique initiation. Brenda felt uneasy, but she had nowhere else to go. That day, Brenda's mother had asked her neighbor to pick up and babysit her daughter after school. Instead, the neighbor sent her two daughters to pick up Brenda. And those daughters, Brenda's babysitters by default, were breaking the law.

"That day, I decided that I didn't want this for me."

One of Brenda's neighbors would end up pregnant by the time she was fourteen. Many of Brenda's other middle school friends would join gangs or end up dead. But not Brenda. She graduated from UCLA and majored in anthropology.

Getting there would not be simple, however.

Coming from El Salvador on TPS status, Brenda's parents had sacrificed everything, and they made sure to remind her of that. "In El Salvador, my dad was an engineer, but here he couldn't get his degrees validated." Because of her parents' sacrifice, Brenda always tried to follow the right path, even while living in a difficult neighborhood.

"I lived in the hood, behind projects in South LA. But to me, it was normal. Until I went to UCLA."

When Brenda went to college, she encountered two worlds within the walls of UCLA. Unlike many of the other students, Brenda had to worry about studying as well as earning an income. Although students could only work part time, she ended up finding ways to work extra hours at Wetzel's Pretzel's, a food franchise within the university. At some point, she was working full time, along with many Central Americans like herself. "I met most of the other Central Americans and Latinos in UCLA while working at Wetzel's Pretzel's.

Money was tight for all of us and we happened to find each other working in the same place!"

Juggling work and school, however, took a toll on Brenda. During the Spring of 2015, she dropped out.

"I was going through mental health issues, the product of overworking and my family's pressure. It was so frustrating—to think that I was just a weird girl who did not fit in and who felt this deep sadness. It was a recipe for disaster."

Despite those struggles, Brenda successfully finished school thanks to determination and the help she received. "Being diagnosed actually brought peace of mind. Before that, I had never really talked about mental health before, with my family or anybody."

Now she is a nurse assistant and is working on nursing school applications, with the purpose of becoming a registered nurse in the future. Helping the migrant community is in her plans too.

"My best friend is a registered nurse, and she is from Ethiopia. She also grew up in the hood; we both would like to benefit our community somehow. We would like to start a nonprofit or an organization that reaches out to immigrants or displaced people who need preventative health when they come to the United States. People with diabetes, high blood pressure, and other conditions. Since being a nurse assistant, I have seen many incidences of hospitalization. We need a healthy community, that's the goal!"

Brenda's decisions in critical junctures of her life steered her towards a life free of the hardships that many of her neighbors and friends experienced. Had she not listened to her parents, things could have turned out differently. Trying to start a life from scratch in another country, as Brenda's parents did, is never easy on anyone—not on the migrants and certainly not on their children.

I always think that Carlos, my dear friend, was lucky enough to be born in a country that offered the option of a good quality education and a platform to thrive in the labor market.

He once visited me in Honduras, and he met someone whose experience resonated with his: a young girl who was attending public university in Honduras. Like him, she wanted to become a lawyer, and she came from a struggling family. However, a key difference set their experiences apart: for long periods, her professors were on strike, so she could not attend class. Consequently, she and her classmates fell behind on class content, and often failed exams that included material they had never covered. This was just one of the many barriers for her to achieve her goals.

When people feel like they cannot grow academically or professionally at home, or are unable to provide for their family, the answer might lie elsewhere.

PART III

WHERE DO WE GO FROM HERE?

CHAPTER 10

#DÓNDE-ESTÁ-EL-DINERO

As I walked through a dirt road and entered the ceramic mint-green walls of the Escuela 21 de Octubre in 2013, a group of energetic third graders circled me in excitement. "Hi teacher, hi teacher!" they yelled, ushering among the few English words they knew. Some tugged at my pants, hungry for attention. Despite my determination to help them learn English, I questioned my ability to successfully do so. After all, I had no teaching experience or training.

In the middle of my senior year, a government directive required bilingual school students to teach English at public schools to complete community service hours needed to graduate. That is how I began teaching English every Saturday at 9 a.m. sharp, without any teaching experience and without any training.

One day, as my classmates and I discussed our teaching experiences, one of them mentioned something that instantly disillusioned me: "You know how they are making us teach English as part of the obligatory community service hours to graduate? Well, apparently a foundation donated money to support English learning programs in Honduran public schools, but the money disappeared. Now the creative way for the government to ensure students are still learning English without spending a dollar is making kids who speak English teach other kids. It's free labor!"

I never confirmed the veracity of my classmate's statement—but believing it is not hard. Government institutions with chronic issues like money mismanagement, failure to execute the budget, and corruption scandals are common in the region. Without proper management, these institutions are unable to function, leaving citizens they are meant to support to fend for themselves. Had my classmate's claim been true, depriving these kids of resources meant to improve their employability, education, and opportunities could have jeopardized their prospects of a better future.

More recently, citizens have questioned the government's spending during the infamous coronavirus (COVID-19) pandemic.

"Fe y Esperanza," a short concrete bridge with a large arch, located only five minutes away from my former neighborhood in Tegucigalpa, now has an imprint for everyone to see. For cars approaching the bridge, it is impossible to look away—right on the bridge's crest, in large bold white letters reads a message to the Honduran government:

"¿DóndeEstáElDinero? #HondurasLoExige" (Where is the Money? Honduras Demands It).[88]

Since the World Health Organization labelled COVID-19 a pandemic, irregularities in the execution of budget aimed at addressing the effects of the virus have upset many Hondurans, explaining why people are requesting to know what happened with the money. During the initial stages in March, the irregularities were very subtle. In later months, they were less so.

Alejandro Kafatti knows the ins and outs of the Honduran government's budget. As an economist for an independent think tank in Honduras, he monitors the government's budget allocations on a weekly basis. We spoke in March of 2020, just as the pandemic picked up speed.

Allocations of money aimed at fighting off or addressing COVID-19, Alejandro explained, had increased. The two government agencies meant to receive these disbursements were the Ministry of Health and the Permanent Commission to Contingency in Honduras (COPECO). Therefore, he expected to find a budgetary increase in the money allocated to these institutions.

These are the chronological changes in budget allocations:

- Mid-February: The National Congress approved 110 million Lempiras (Honduran currency, equivalent to

---

88   Damaris Torres, "Honduras: escriben en puente Fe y Esperanza, ¿Dónde está el dinero, #Honduras lo exige?" *Radio HRN,* August 2020.

approximately $4.425 million) to combat dengue and future positive cases of COVID-19, allocated to COPECO.

- Two days later: Approximately 200 million more Lempiras were approved to combat COVID-19 cases in the country (approximately $8.01 million).
- March 5: The country's health authorities witnessed the first positive case, so the government requested an additional 602 billion Lempiras ($24.138 million) through the executive branch of the National Congress to combat COVID-19.
- March 7: The administrative council solicited the National Congress to approve $402 million for the construction of ninety clinics and hospital nationwide with the purpose of combatting COVID-19 and creating a new health system. This money came from the Honduran Social Security Institute.

However, as part of his weekly monitoring exercise, he checked whether the Secretariat of Finance or other entity had disbursed the allocated money to these institutions. They hadn't.

"I had to report the following information to my supervisor: Even though the National Congress allocated resources to fighting COVID-19, an initiative led by the Ministry of Health and COPECO, these government entities had not received any money. The last disbursements happened in December 2019 and January 2020, before COVID-19. Meanwhile, the National Congress had been approving resources precisely to combat COVID-19 since mid-February to these institutions. They just weren't getting the funds."

Alejandro quickly pointed out that it would be unfair to blame politicians for stealing it all—rather, he believes the money never existed in the first place.

"I think it was symbolic money, money that only existed in paper. In other words, maybe the current account balance was not exact, and they were trying to adjust it or something. This means that this money never reached neither the Ministry of Health or COPECO, or any other institution meant to help Hondurans confront this worldwide pandemic. Meanwhile people are dying."

Since then, the Ministry of Health had confirmed twelve new cases, increasing the total number to twenty four cases.

Months after my conversation with Alejandro, the media caught on to more irregularities related to purchases aimed to help alleviate the effects of COVID-19. The government of Honduras purchased seven mobile hospitals intended to treat COVID-19 patients and valued at forty-eight million dollars (USD). To date, only two of those mobile hospitals made it to Honduras.[89] That's when the real outrage began, and that's the reason why now, in the middle of the city, you find those white words, as well as the hashtags #DondeEstáElDinero and #HondurasLoExige on several thousand social media accounts. People demand to know where the money went.

Whether this is a case of corruption, money mismanagement, or inability to execute the budget is hard to determine. What

---

89   Ana Melgar, "Fiscalía de Honduras investiga posible fraude en compra de hospitales móviles para atender pacientes de covid-19," *CNN*, June 2020.

is clear, however, is that somewhere along the way, taxpayers' money is ending up nowhere, and citizens are the ones who suffer.

In Guatemala, the government entity in charge of protecting migrants and coordinating reintegration service to returnees suffers from poor capacity to execute its budget. The National Council of Attention to Migrants of Guatemala (Conamigua) only executed 12 percent of its 2017 budget, 23 percent in 2018, and 22 percent in 2019.[90]

Amid the COVID-19 crisis, migrants have been among the most vulnerable groups, and Conamigua's responsibilities have increased. Conamigua invested eight million quetzales (approximately one million dollars) in reception, transportation, and lodging to accommodate 452 migrants deported from Mexico and 344 from the United States during the pandemic.[91] These high expenses are mostly related to new sanitary protocols in place. Meanwhile, the lack of capacity to support migrants remained a problem. According to Conamigua's executive subsecretary, María Elizondo Hernández, the failure to execute their budget is due to lack of human resources, with only eleven people supporting procurement processes, and poor planning by the previous secretary in charge.[92] The failures have been so severe that the Minister

---

90 José Pablo Del Águila, "Conamigua tiene una pobre ejecución de presupuesto en doce años de vida," *Prensa Libre,* September 17, 2020.

91 Sergio Morales Rodas, "Recepción de migrantes deportados ha costado más de Q8.4 millones,"*Prensa Libre,* August 10, 2020.

92 Sergio Morales Rodas, "Recepción de migrantes deportados ha costado más de Q8.4 millones."

of Foreign Affairs, Pedro Brolo, has suggested dissolving the institution altogether.

Honduras seems to have centers that suffer from little capacity as well. Approximately five years ago, I spoke to a nun who ran a migration reception center in Honduras. The nun complained endlessly on the lack of resources she had to receive returning migrants. She had been calling the government entities pleading for more funds or human resources because they could not deal with the large volume of migrants they received. Despite the center's important role in helping returnees reintegrate into society, I cannot find the migration center anymore on the internet or anywhere else.

What happens to the people who return to a country with no economic opportunities and institutions that are so weak that they cannot support them? According to a report by the Migration Policy Institute, addressing the needs of returning migrants is essential; returnees find themselves in a saturated and competitive labor market that often crowds out migrants, forcing them to work in the informal sector.[93] Furthermore, deportees in El Salvador, Guatemala, and Honduras experience stigmatization or employment discrimination, particularly in El Salvador where young returnees with piercings or tattoos are less likely to find employment in the formal sector

---

93   Ariel G. Ruiz Soto, Rodrigo Dominguez-Villegas, Luis Argueta, and Randy Capps, "Sustainable Reintegration: Strategies to Support Migrants Returning to Mexico and Central America," *Migration Policy Institute,* January 2019: 23.

due to the employer's perceptions that they were criminals or gang members.[94]

Lack of technical capacity or human resources is part of the chronic issues found in government institutions. Paired with rampant cases of corruption that drain the already scarce resources, the institutions meant to support people are further debilitated.

Corruption is one of the best known problems in Central America. The Corruption Perceptions Index (CPI) is a measure of citizens' perception of corruption in a country, developed by Transparency International. It is a composite index, as it combines different international surveys and assessment of corruption collected by a variety of reputable institutions. A CPI of close to 0 indicates that the public sector is perceived to be highly corrupt; a value close to 100 indicates that it is perceived to not be corrupt.

According to the Corruption Perceptions Index in 2019, Costa Rica is the highest-ranked Central American country, at 44 out of 180 countries.[95] Every other country scored lower, with Guatemala and Honduras being tied, and Nicaragua being the lowest.

---

94 Ariel G. Ruiz Soto, Rodrigo Dominguez-Villegas, Luis Argueta, and Randy Capps, "Sustainable Reintegration: Strategies to Support Migrants Returning to Mexico and Central America," 24.

95 "Corruption Perceptions Index," Transparency International, accessed February 15, 2020.

Corruption Perceptions Index (CPI) 2019		
Country	CPI score 2019	Rank
Costa Rica	56	44
El Salvador	34	113
Guatemala	26	146
Honduras	26	146
Nicaragua	22	161
Source: "Corruption Perceptions Index," Transparency International, accessed February 15, 2020.		

Although the CPI index is only a proxy of people's perceptions of corruption rather than a real measure of corruption itself, it has validity in terms of what people experience on a day-to-day basis.

The Migration Policy Institute looked at the relationship between CPI scores, and the net migration rate (the number of immigrants minus the number of emigrants per one thousand people) for 174 countries and territories in 2015. Countries where corruption was perceived to be more of an issue were primarily countries from which people emigrated, while those where corruption was perceived as less of an issue were countries where people immigrated to.[96] This is in no way as a sign of causality, but rather as a pattern or tendency that is worth noting, especially when corruption means a worse livelihood for its citizens in terms of social security or other basic services.

---

96   Jørgen Carling, Erlend Paasche, and Melissa Siege. "Finding Connections: The Nexus between Migration and Corruption," *Migration Policy Institute,* (May 2015).

In 2015, both Honduras and Guatemala faced some of the largest corruption scandals ever witnessed in the region.

The United Nations established the anti-corruption body CICIG on December 12, 2006, at the request of the Guatemalan government. As an independent entity, its purpose was to support the Public Prosecutor's Office, the National Civilian Police, and other state institutions in the investigation of crimes committed by illegal groups and clandestine security structures. Soon enough, the CICIG dismantled a wide corruption network deep within the government structures, including within the social security system aimed at protecting Guatemalans.[97]

For approximately a year, bribes had been collected from businessmen and users of different customs in the country in exchange for modifying what importers had to pay to the treasury, or what is called the Superintendency of Tax Administration (Superintendencia de Administración Tributaria, or SAT).[98] The SAT is equivalent to the Internal Revenue Service in the United States, so you can imagine how outraged people were.

On April of 2015, the CICIG unraveled that corruption network, one that implicated many government officials, including President Otto Pérez Molina and Vice President Roxana Baldetti, the masterminds behind the operation.

---

97 Kristel Mucino, "WOLA Report on the International Commission against Impunity in Guatemala (CICIG)," *WOLA* (June 2015: 8-9).
98 Kristel Mucino, "WOLA Report on the International Commission against Impunity in Guatemala (CICIG)" 22-23.

The CICIG would later ask for the impeachment of President Pérez Molina and the arrest of Vice President Baldetti. Historic protests broke out, with thousands of Guatemalans demanding that both the president and vice president step down. Soon afterward, the president was impeached and the vice president imprisoned.

A month after this scandal involving the SAT and the country's two main leaders, the CICIG uncovered a second scandal. They found that the board of directors of the Guatemalan Social Security Institute (Instituto Guatemalteco de Seguridad Social, or IGSS) had changed its supplier of kidney dialysis treatment to a Mexican firm, PISA, awarding it a $15.67 million. According to CICIG wiretaps, IGSS employees, businessmen, and the head of the Bank of Guatemala would make 15 to 16 percent of the contract in kickbacks.[99] The poor quality of the kidney dialysis treatment provided by the firm resulted in the death of five kidney failure patients.[100]

Around the same time, Honduras experienced its own corruption scandal: the National Health System scandal. Just like in the case of Guatemala, the entity meant to serve people with proper healthcare had failed them.

Everything began in 2009, when Mario Zelaya, a reputable and renowned orthopedist, earned the position of head of the Honduran Social Security Institute (IHSS). In August of 2013, someone anonymously complained of a surcharge of air tickets, in the name of Mario Zelaya and other officials of

99   Nic Wirtz, "Corruption Network in Guatemalan Health System Exposed," *Americas Quarterly,* May 22, 2015.
100 Nic Wirtz, "Corruption Network in Guatemalan Health System Exposed."

the IHSS, which had been made in May of 2011.[101] It seemed like just confusion, maybe even an accident. However, the initial suspicion led to an investigation that would unfold into something much deeper than anyone could have initially imagined.

The investigation found that, along with two other officials, a complex embezzlement and bribery network had emptied at least two hundred million US dollars from the IHSS in a time range of five years.[102] That's right—two hundred million dollars that could have and should have been used for the healthcare and retirement of Honduran citizens.

In 2014, Mario Zelaya stepped down from his post, and in April of that year, he received an arrest warrant. He went into hiding for some time, and my classmates and I constantly chatted about it: "I wonder where he is hiding? I hope they find him soon. He deserves all the jail time in the world." Authorities caught him a couple of months later and threw him into prison.

The President at the time, Juan Orlando Hernández, spoke about Mario Zelaya's arrest as a prideful moment: "This arrest is a forceful demonstration of the diligent and effective functioning of the security and defense institutions of the State." Perhaps in the moment it seemed like an honest and truthful diagnosis: the fact that Mario Zelaya had indeed

---

101 *BBC News*, "El escándalo que llevó al ejército a controlar los medicamentos en Honduras" (June 19, 2015).

102 BBC News"El escándalo que llevó al ejército a controlar los medicamentos en Honduras."

been found and caught seemed to indicate that the state had the necessary measures to contain widespread corruption.

But the story does not end there (unfortunately). In 2015, new information implicated the president in this scandal too. Almost $135,000 had been paid in checks that contributed to President Hernández's campaign in 2013, which came from companies that had received money from the IHSS during Mario Zelaya's administration. Although the President claimed that he never realized where the money came from, citizens were outraged.

For approximately three months, Hondurans peacefully marched in an event later coined the "torchlight march." Through these marches, the protesters were demanding two things: that the president step down and the creation of an international commission against impunity like the CICIG in Guatemala.

Corruption, money mismanagement, and poor technical capacity within government institutions affects people's livelihood. It can affect people like my third-grade students trying to learn English while stuck with an incompetent teacher like myself rather than a professional, or the returning migrants who are among the most vulnerable groups during the pandemic. In the case of Guatemala, corruption literally caused the death of people. These are the chronic issues that make citizens constantly wonder where government institutions' money is and how it is being used—they demand to know.

CHAPTER 11

LOCATION, LOCATION, LOCATION

Just off the dusty dirt road to Los Encinitos, a humble, cinder-block building seems to emerge out of nowhere. The absence of storefronts, restaurants, and residences in the area provides a hint to the vital role the unassuming building plays throughout this remote, hillside neighborhood.

When I lived in Honduras, I made the thirty-three-mile (fifty-three-kilometer) trip from my family's home in Tegucigalpa to Los Encinitos by car. The drive follows a rough, narrow, unpaved road. Most visitors traverse it by donkey or by foot. It's a challenging trek, but it's a small price for them to pay for access to medical and dental care.

Doctors and volunteers from CAPE CARES, a non-profit humanitarian organization, provide primary healthcare services at Los Encinitos and a handful of other rural, underserved Honduran communities like it—communities that would otherwise have no access to medical care. Physicians and medical school students come from around the world to volunteer their time and services. As a high school student, I served as a translator between the local patients and the visiting doctors from the United States and the United Kingdom.

Traveling throughout Central America, I have stumbled upon similar remote towns. People living in these territories are the hardest to reach. And yet, sometimes they are the people who need the most support and attention.

Had CAPE CARES operated in the capital city of Tegucigalpa, where there are plenty of clinics and public hospitals, rather than Los Encinitos, I would have been dumbfounded. Strategies that attempt to curb migration, or the factors related to migration such as violence, often neglect this reality. They target places like Tegucigalpa where the issues are not as relevant, whereas places like San Marcos and Los Encinitos are forgotten.

Rafael Jerez, renowned Honduran lawyer, journalist, and member of the Association for a More Just Society (ASJ), analyzes issues of transparency, human rights, and impunity. The topics covered during our chat reinforced the differences between municipalities.

His team updated the Homicide Impunity Index in Honduras, using a simple equation: the number of homicides that did not end in a conviction divided by the total number of homicides in a given year. It provided a proxy of the proportion of homicides that do not successfully get convicted. They calculated the index for national and departmental levels.

In 2012, the index at the national level was 96 percent, a high number given that Honduras had reached its highest peak of homicides: 86.5 homicides per 100,000 inhabitants, or a 181 percent increase in a period of seven years. This meant that despite the high number of homicides, 96 percent had not received any conviction by the country's judicial authorities.[103]

Five years later, the index had decreased to 87 percent, a 9-percent decrease. To Rafael and his team, this seemed like an improvement; it appeared that more homicide cases were leading to a conviction in the criminal justice system. In fact, he mentioned that the Honduran government had been boasting this improvement in reducing impunity, an issue that Honduras is often condemned for.

Homicide Impunity Index				
Year	Homicides	Convictions	Homicides not convicted	Index
2010	6,239	222	6,017	96%
2011	7,104	298	6,806	96%
2012	7,172	279	6,893	96%
2013	6,757	298	6,459	96%
2014	5,936	495	5,441	92%
2015	5,148	412	4,736	92%
2016	5,150	448	4,702	91%
2017	3,866	491	3,375	87%

Source: Alianza por la Justicia y la Paz, 2019.

---

103 Lester Ramírez Irías and Rafael Jerez Moreno, "Informe sobre la impunidad en homicidios: Periodo de estudio 2010-2017," *Alianza por la Paz y la Justicia,* June 2019 :19

The index, however, told only part of the story. To find out what was really happening, Rafael would have to delve deeper into the data. By disaggregating the data by department level, he could get a better picture of the distribution of homicide convictions across the country's territories. The data baffled him. While homicide impunity rates did steadily decline in the two largest areas in the country, the picture in the rest of Honduras stood in stark contrast. Communities across the northern territories—fully one third of the country—experienced a surge in homicide impunity, with 90 percent of all homicide cases ending without a conviction.

According to Rafael's boss, these northern territories also had the highest rates of emigration in the country. They believed drug trafficking and gang violence fueled out-migration in these territories, but lack of resources and restrictions from entering those zones made their speculations impossible to confirm. Addressing migration is difficult because it does not just happen from one country to another. It happens from a specific municipality, geared by those municipalities' conditions.

The US-led Plan for the Alliance for Prosperity (A4P) is heavily invested in efforts to curb out-migration in portions of the Northern Triangle. When administrators of A4P developed their investment strategy, however, they only selected municipalities with low migration rates (with the exception of Honduras), as seen below.

Key Indicators in A4P Selected Municipalities			
	El Salvador	Guatemala	Honduras
Migrants	19%	11%	84%
Child/Youth Migrants	25%	54%	81%

Source: Manuel Orozco, "One Step Forward for Central America: The Plan for the Alliance for Prosperity," The Inter-American Dialogue, March 16, 2016.

Only 19 percent of adult migrants and 25 percent of child migrants came from the municipalities chosen in El Salvador. In Guatemala, although 54 percent of child migrants were from the chosen municipalities, only 11 percent of adult migrants were.[104] In other words, there seemed to be a disconnect between the selected municipalities, and the intensity of the problems. Consequently, the funds and support failed to reach the municipalities most characterized by out-migration and, therefore, most in need of intervention.

By throwing money at a problem without first identifying where the problem existed, the A4P wasted resources and left vulnerable municipalities to fend for themselves. In Los Angeles' fight against gang violence, the county encountered similar failures before finding a solution.

Los Angeles spent twenty-five billion dollars to eliminate gang violence during a bloody thirty-year period. The birthplace of gangs that would later expand to Central America, L.A. saw gang-related homicides quadruple from 1982 to

---

104 Manuel Orozco, "One Step Forward for Central America: The Plan for the Alliance for Prosperity," *The Inter-American Dialogue*, March 16, 2016.

1992.[105] Connie Rice, a lawyer and activist, wanted to find a solution.

Crime, Connie says, paired with policing tactics that perpetrated violent behavior, led to a buildup of tensions between the Los Angeles Police Department (LAPD), the L.A. community, and gang members.

In an interview with NPR, she described waking up every day for two decades "trying to figure out a new way to sue the LAPD and the L.A. County Sheriffs, because they were such a negative and humiliating and emasculating force in the black and brown communities."[106] Tension grew so extreme between Connie and the police, she said, that the Police Protective League actually physically removed her from buildings.[107]

The LAPD and Connie Rice shared a common goal: to end the gang war that had taken a toll on the L.A. community and had cost the county so much money. The methodology, however, differed.

Not unlike the Central American governments' war on gang violence, the LAPD's strategy included repressive tactics such as the militarization of police and massive incarcerations. The fact that these measures had not contributed to a

---

105 Karen Umemoto, *The Truce : Lessons from an L.A. Gang War* (Ithaca, NY: Cornell University Press, 2018), 59.

106 Connie Rice, "Civil Rights Attorney On How She Built Trust With Police," interview by NPR Staff, *Code Sw!tch*, NPR, December 5, 2014. Audio, MP3, 7:03.

107 Patt Morison, "Patt Morrison Asks: Connie Rice,"*Los Angeles Times*, December 28, 2011.

reduction in homicides and deaths came as no surprise to critics like Connie.

"The last thing L.A. needed was more militarization."[108]

In her book, *Power Concedes Nothing,* Connie recounts, "After a thirty-year, twenty-five-billion-dollar war on gangs, L.A. had racked up an impressive scorecard of a million arrests—but also six times as many gangs and enough gang violence to alarm the World Health Organization. 'War' had boosted the number of gangs and done nothing to stop the spread of gang ideology, influence, and power."[109]

Despite initial tensions with the LAPD, Connie conducted a landmark eighteen-month assessment of the city of Los Angeles' anti-gang programs along with the LAPD. In January of 2007, Connie's public policy change organization, the Advancement Project's Urban Peace program, released its groundbreaking report: "A Call to Action: A Case for a Comprehensive Solution to L.A.'s Gang Violence Epidemic." The report put forth a comprehensive set of over 106 recommendations to change the paradigm, operation, and strategy for combating gang violence. The community-based approach recognized the complexities of why youth and other community members engaged in violence, including individual, societal, and economic factors.[110]

---

108 Connie Rice, *Power Concedes Nothing: The Unfinished Fight for Social Justice* (New York: Scribner, 2014), 4.

109 Connie Rice, *Power Concedes Nothing: The Unfinished Fight for Social Justice,* 4.

110 "A Call to Action: Los Angeles' Quest to Achieve Community Safety," *Advancement Project,* n.d: 13.

Five years after the LAPD implemented the new policies, gang-related crime tanked by over 15 percent. In key neighborhoods, gang-related homicides fell by 35 percent.[111]

Understanding the community's circumstances and including several stakeholders constituted important pillars in Connie's approach. A similar approach might not have been successful in another location with different stakeholders, actors, and necessities.

Unfortunately, the areas where the most vulnerable people often live, places like Los Encinitos, are often the most disregarded by Central American governments.

---

111 "A Call to Action: Los Angeles' Quest to Achieve Community Safety," *Advancement Project*, n.d: 4.

CHAPTER 12

A PORTAL TO CENTRAL AMERICA

———

Entering El Progreso Market in Washington, DC's, Mount Pleasant neighborhood is like returning to a local *pulpería*, or small convenience store, near my family's home in Honduras. Stacked to the brim on every shelf, the familiar packaging is as comforting as the comfort food inside.

I first happened upon this oasis of Latin goods by chance. I might have walked right past it if not for a small banner falling from a pole above a store's entrance. *VERDURAS, FRUTAS, CARNES* in bold, red letters, all in Spanish. A second, smaller sign advertised *Envío de Dinero*, literally translated to "money sending."

Once inside the small, cramped store, I spotted a display of Natura's refried beans. I picked up a bag and suddenly nostalgia set in. In all the years I had lived in DC, I'd had no luck finding them in any of the grocery markets and big box retail stores. But there they were, in this small congested space, a taste of home.

Just like a portal, when entering the Progreso Market, Central Americans are transported home in the blink of an eye. That's why they go there—to connect to their country by purchasing local products while sending money transfers to their loved ones.

These local products are called nostalgia goods, precisely because they elicit that sense of belonging for people who miss their home country. Demand for these products is high: a 2008 survey conducted by the Inter-American Dialogue of 1,300 migrants in the United States showed that approximately 90 percent consumed home goods.[112] In El Salvador, among the most cited nostalgia products are different types of local cheeses (such as *cuajada*), mango, and other local fruit like jocote. The 90 percent of migrants from El Salvador who purchase nostalgia goods spend an average of $137 a month (or $1,644 a year) on these goods. This is 42 percent of local consumption.

Of the migrants who consume home-country goods, 40 percent report that they have had difficulty finding certain products. Facilitating channels for nostalgia goods to reach the market in the United States, especially those smaller producers, is a great opportunity for economic development at home. In addition, places like El Progreso Market, can benefit from having a wider variety of products for their clientele.

---

112 Manuel Orozco and Julia Yansura, "A Taste of Home: The Nostalgia Trade and Migrant Economic Transnationalism," *Inter-American Dialogue.*

Another way to reconnect to home is through money transfers. Before the pandemic started, I took an Uber with a driver from El Salvador who spoke to me in Spanish after realizing my name was Catalina. As we chatted, he explained that he came to the United States to generate income and send it back home. "In the US, even though I work and work and work until I am exhausted, at least I am making money. In El Salvador, I worked even more, and it was never enough. That's why I came here, so I could make money, and send it back home to my family every month." He supports his family by transferring funds through places like El Progreso or other convenience stores that offer that service.

These money flows from the United States to Central American countries compete with international aid as one of the largest financial inflows. For instance, in 2018 they represented 20.7 percent of El Salvador's GDP, 20.1 percent of Honduras' GDP, and 12.1 percent of Guatemala's GDP. This is high, particularly compared to the rest of Latin American countries, for which remittances constitute less than 2 percent of GDP on average.[113]

Not only are these sums large, but they have also grown throughout the years. The volume of remittances increased in 2019, particularly in Guatemala (by 13.1 percent) and Honduras (by 14 percent) compared to the previous year. This increase is higher than in other countries with a large

---

113 Emmanuel Abuelafia, Giselle Del Carmen, Marta Ruiz-Arranz, "Tras los pasos del migrante: Perspectivas y experiencias de la migración de El Salvador, Guatemala y Honduras en Estados Unidos," *Inter-American Development Bank* (December 2019: 24).

migrant population in the United States, like Mexico (7 percent).[114]

The transfers—commonly known as remittances—play an important role in the economies of Central American countries.

As an intern at the Inter-American Dialog one summer, I worked on a project to rate remittance companies, publishing the results in a Remittances Scorecard report. My team and I used a quantitative framework including twelve indicators, such as geographical coverage, product offerings, payment networks, transfer costs, and customer service to rate these companies.[115] To assess customer service, for instance, I had to go undercover, posing as a granddaughter who wished to send five hundred dollars to my *abuelito* in El Salvador.

The scorecard's motive was simple: by rating remittance companies, we forced them to compete with their rivals by offering better services. For customers like the Uber driver who wished to send money to his family at the lowest cost possible, this type of competition is helpful.

Brenda's family, from Chapters 4 and 9, used to send money to El Salvador too. Although her dad earned five dollars an hour at work, he was committed to supporting Brenda's grandparents. "My dad sent three hundred or four hundred dollars each month to them, and I always questioned his

---

114 Manuel Orozco, "Remittances to Latin America and the Caribbean: Emerging Challenges: 2019," *Inter-American Dialogue*, 2019: 4.
115 Manuel Orozco, Laura Porras, Julia Yansura, "Remittances Scorecard: 2016," *Inter-American Dialogue*, December 16, 2016.

decision. When kids at school threw away their food, I was always horrified because we barely had enough money to buy food at home. Meanwhile, my father was sending money to my grandparents. Now I understand why we needed to help them. My grandparents didn't have stable jobs. My grandfather sometimes farmed or did construction work. But those three or four hundred dollars were their main source of income." To Brenda's grandparents, the Uber driver's family, and other Central Americans, sending money at lower costs is essential to supporting their family at home.

In 2019, a tweet by President Trump threatened to tax remittances if Guatemala's migration to the United States continued, something that could raise the cost of sending remittances, limiting their flow to Guatemala. Furthermore, Trump has threatened to tax remittances to make Mexico pay for the border wall. Although none of these happened, they could have threatened the livelihood of people who depend on these transfers, worsening conditions at home.

Despite their importance for Central American households, the discussion of whether remittances support or inhibit development in the region is ongoing.

Tim Gindling, PhD in economics from Cornell University, conducts research on labor economics in Central America. He has analyzed the impact of migration and remittances on labor markets. "Remittances are mostly good in terms of public investment, and financing human capital accumulation," he said. "One potential negative in the literature is that the availability of remittances could lead to a decrease in labor force participation at home, and more self-employment."

This is not necessarily bad, Dr. Gindling said, but one should take it into consideration when formulating policies.

As others have pointed out, considered alone, remittances are a symptom of disparate opportunities among countries. But coupled with the right incentive framework, they can be an important resource for the development of poor countries.[116]

Others echo the belief that remittances can have a positive impact if the proper strategy is used. Ariel Ruiz, policy analyst at the Migration Policy Institute in Washington, DC, commented on the role of remittances and development: "Remittances are an incredible mechanism to increase development in the region, perhaps more than any other, while at the same time incentivizing or complicating issues of internal development. In an ideal scenario, what should occur is that remittances continue to be an important factor in the development and improvement of migrants in poor countries, but are also accompanied by significant transparent investment as part of these approaches."

A discussion on ways to use these transfers not only to support households, but to support development in home countries, has emerged in academic and policy circles.

Dr. Manuel Orozco has researched migration and development for two decades. As director of the Center for Migration and Economic Stabilization at Creative Associates International, he has found ways to use nostalgia trade and

116 Donald F. Terry and Steven R. Wilson, "Beyond Small Change: Making Migrant Remittances Count," *Inter-American Development Bank*, 2005.

remittances as platforms for development in Central American countries.

Although remittances alone amounted to seventeen billion dollars in 2015, or nearly 50 percent of income in some 3.5 million households in the region, the majority is informal, "under the mattress" savings.[117] Thus, Manuel's team conducted pilot programs in Guatemala and Nicaragua by partnering up with local institutions, banks, or credit union branches with a high percentage of customers receiving remittances, and offered financial literacy workshops, teaching them how to enroll in the formal banking system, save or invest in future projects using remittance transfers.[118]

"In parts of Guatemala, we have linked remittances to economic growth," Orozco explained, "Through the financial literacy workshops, we can develop a strategy that involves human capital investment, reduces informality, and increases savings capitalization, all based on the transfer of remittances. Based on our estimations, these projects can increase economic growth by at least 1.5 percent in these countries."

What's more, these projects can also economically support households in Central America, reducing the need to migrate for some people. His evaluation shows that for households that have accounts and have deposited their remittance money into those accounts (in other words, formalized their

---

117 Manuel Orozco, "One Step Forward for Central America: The Plan for the Alliance for Prosperity," *Inter-American Dialogue*, March 16, 2016.

118 Manuel Orozco and Julia Yansura, "Remittances and Financial Inclusion: Opportunities for Central America," *Inter-American Dialogue*, February 1, 2015.

savings), the probability that a family member migrated in the last twelve months is half that of those who live in households that have not formalized their savings.[119]

"Access to financial products and financial services is one of the most important aspects that influences that intersection between migration and development. And nobody really pays attention to it."

Several studies, including in other countries, have shown how remittances can help not only household welfare, but also other social aspects, such as education. For instance, a study in Mexico shows how literacy among children ages six to fourteen improved significantly among families that received higher levels of remittances, while school attendance levels improved for those ages thirteen to fifteen.[120] This has also been seen in cases closer to the Central American countries: El Salvador. In El Salvador, even modest remittances drastically have reduced the likelihood of a family's children dropping out of school.[121]

Places like the Progreso Market are important because they are a portal to Central America, a place where Central Americans can channel resources to their home countries either by purchasing nostalgia goods or sending money transfers.

---

119 "Proyecto Oportunidades para mi Comunidad," *USAID* and *Inter-American Dialogue,* July 2019.
120 Ernesto Lopez-Cordova, and Alexandra Olmedo, "International Remittances and Development: Existing Evidence, Policies and Recommendations,"*INTAL/ITD Occasional Paper,*no. 41 (January 2006).
121 Anthony L. Hall, "Migrant Remittances, Livelihood, and Development," in *Moving Away from Poverty,* ed. Deepa Narayan, Patti Petesch (Washington DC, World Bank, 2007):315.

Paired with public policies or projects, they could be a portal to development in the region as well.

CHAPTER 13

YOU CAN'T JUDGE A COWBOY BY HIS HAT

———

What is good and what is evil? In old Western movies, the good cowboys wear white hats. They are heroes, sitting atop their horses riding along a dirt road during a scorching hot day, armed with rifles and revolvers. Often, they are the winners, beating the bad guys in combat and victoriously riding away. The bad guys, on the other hand, wear black hats.

In real life, identifying who is good and who is bad is not as simple.

As if taken from a cowboy film, the then-president Manuel "Mel" Zelaya was the splitting image of the good guy. He wore a large white cowboy hat, often rode a horse, and displayed a thick dark mustache—his trademark image. Unlike most Honduran authority figures, Mel Zelaya never obtained a college degree, a source of criticism from the opposition. He was a left-leaning president who catered to middle- and lower-class citizens, making him the good guy to many Hondurans.

In 2009, tensions rose as Mel Zelaya attempted to pass a referendum to change the constitution, allowing him to run for a second term. The Honduran constitution permanently outlaws presidential reelection, so many people disapproved of the president's actions. Manuel Zelaya's intentions to remain in power seemed like the first red flag, blurring the lines between good and evil.

The opposition, furious at the president for abusing his power, questioned his attempts to change the constitution. His supporters, on the other hand, condemned the opposition for not allowing the president to exert his self-proclaimed right to remain in power. Other countries allowed reelection—why couldn't Honduras be the same? As the situation escalated between both sides, my parents decided it was best if we spent some time away from Honduras.

It was my birthday—June 27—when my family and I hopped on a plane and took a quick forty-minute flight to Costa Rica. I felt such a thrill to spend my birthday with family and a relief to leave Honduras for a couple of weeks.

Little did we know that Honduras was mere hours away from a constitutional crisis.

One day after my fourteenth birthday, everything changed for my country. I awoke in Costa Rica that morning to the sound of my mother's voice.

"Catalina, you have to come watch the news!"

I sprinted to the living room in my pajamas and stared at the television, stunned by what I saw. The Honduran military had kidnapped President Zelaya in the middle of the night, shoved him into an airplane against his will, and flown him to Costa Rica. He was still wearing his pajamas.

My family joked, saying, "It seems like the president is following us!" Although it seemed funny at first, we expected negative repercussions. That same day, the National Congress voted to remove Zelaya and replaced him with Roberto Micheletti, the President of Congress at the time.

The event was labelled a coup d'état because of the military's involvement, although the term has since been disputed. There's no disputing, however, that the event was a constitutional crisis. The secretary general of the Organization of American States (OAS), one of the most important organizations representing Latin American states, suspended Honduras' membership after deeming the event unconstitutional. To Honduras as a country, this meant it had no representation within the organization.

Despite the turmoil, things settled down after several months, prompting us to take a flight back to our home in Tegucigalpa. However, as I rode from the airport to my house, I encountered a different Tegucigalpa. People had taken their fury to the streets in protest: fire, graffiti, and chaos everywhere.

Imagine my surprise, years later, when a WikiLeaks report found that all along, the US had pushed the OAS for new elections in Honduras, a tactic to sideline Zelaya.[122] In other words, the US had actively taken a stand against Mel Zelaya.

However, what happened years later surpassed that initial shock.

In November of 2017, a right-wing Honduran president, Juan Orlando Hernández, attempted what Manuel Zelaya had failed to do: he ran for a second term, without any referendum, without any consultation, without anyone's permission. And he won the elections, albeit fraudulently. The opposition, led by Salvador Nasralla, had been winning until the online ballot tabulation system mysteriously stopped working. Transmission of results were not reactivated until 1:30 a.m. the next day—and by then, Nasralla had lost his lead while the system went down.

Shortly afterwards, the OAS invited Georgetown University professor and statistician Irfan Nooruddin to analyze real-time data on the Honduran elections and conclude whether the results had, indeed, been fraudulent. Professor Nooruddin, who had also been my instructor at Georgetown, concluded:

"The Honduran national election of 2017 experienced a dramatic vote swing away from the opposition alliance and towards the incumbent national party. This analysis raises doubts about the plausibility of such a reversal of fortunes. If one believes the vote tallies to be accurate, it is plausible to

---

122 Nina Lakhani, "Did Hillary Clinton stand by as Honduras coup ushered in era of violence?" *The Guardian*, August 31, 2016.

have such a swing. But the pattern of votes, particularly in turnout rates, is suspicious…There's a marked break in the data that is hard to explain as pure chance. On the basis of this analysis, I would reject the proposition that the National Party won the election legitimately."[123]

In short, he questioned the legitimacy of the election. For supporters of democracy, President Juan Orlando Hernández became a villain in the story. But he was a hero to other Hondurans because he saved the country from leftist policies that could make Honduras another communist Venezuela. Regardless of the side you sat on, the events had unbalanced the already weak region. In this case, Juan Orlando fit the US government's mold of an ideal candidate, whereas Manuel Zelaya had left-leaning tendencies. So when Juan Orlando stayed in power, they supported it.

In this cowboy movie, it turns out that Mel Zelaya wasn't really the protagonist, nor was Juan Orlando Hernández. They were puppets of another character, one that had loitered in the background for a long time: the United States. Sometimes it wore the white hat by providing assistance to Central American countries, pouring money through the Alliance for Prosperity to curb migration. And sometimes—but always behind closed doors—the US wore the black hat.

History is filled with seldom-told stories of tacit interventions by the United States and their destabilizing effect on Central America. In the Cold War context, the US defended

---

123 Irfan Nooruddin, "Analysis for the Organization of American States (OAS)," *Organization of American States,*2017.

right-leaning leaders, often military-backed ones, at the expense of the people living in those countries. Look back at the efforts of President Dwight Eisenhower and his administration, who some might say meddled in Guatemala's domestic affairs.

It was June 27, 1954. Guatemalan president Jacobo Arbenz Guzmán had announced his resignation.[124] But he had not done so willingly.

In the days leading up to his resignation, the Liberation Army—a band of peasant soldiers—helped Colonel Carlos Castillo Armas invade Guatemala, establishing a military government under his command.[125] Colonel Castillo Armas and his Liberation Army were puppets of the United States. They had received logistical support from the CIA through a covert operation, dubbed Operation PBSUCCESS and authorized by President Eisenhower. The covert ops came with a $2.7 million budget, earmarked for psychological warfare, political action, and subversion for communists and collaborators.[126] But President Arbenz was hardly a communist. He was a nationalist, fending for his country's interests rather than bowing to imperialist powers.[127] In the eyes of many

---

124 Stephen M. Streeter, "Interpreting the 1954 U.S. Intervention in Guatemala: Realist, Revisionist, and Postrevisionist Perspectives," *The History Teacher*, Vol. 34, No. 1 (Nov 2000: 61).

125 Stephen M. Streeter, "Interpreting the 1954 U.S. Intervention in Guatemala: Realist, Revisionist, and Postrevisionist Perspectives," 61.

126 Kate Doyle and Peter Kornbluh, "CIA and Assassinations: The Guatemala 1954 Documents," *National Security Archive Electronic Briefing*, Book No. 4.

127 Stephen M. Streeter, "Interpreting the 1954 U.S. Intervention in Guatemala: Realist, Revisionist, and Postrevisionist Perspectives," 62.

in Guatemala, he wore the white hat. But in protection of his own country's interests, he had crossed an American corporation with plantations in Guatemala. Wealthy planters and officials from the United Fruit Company, enraged by President Arbenz's 1952 land reform program, Decree 900, sought revenge. All it took to make the Guatemalan president a perceived enemy of the US was a propaganda campaign tagging him as a Communist.[128] After the attack and over-throw, he was exiled. With recognition by the United States government, Colonel Castillo proclaimed himself President.

Eisenhower failed to understand Arbenz's motive was in defense of his country, not a communist ideology. He sought to become a protagonist in his own country, without strings attached to other powers. Today, many Hondurans refer to Arbenz as a martyr to US imperialism.

Today, we also know about the role of some bad actors in the plot to overthrow Arbenz. Years after the attack, declas-sified documents reveal that the CIA of the early 1950s had prepared an assassination list. The names of intended targets during the operation against Arbenz had been divided into two categories: key communist personnel to be disposed through "executive action" (killing), and others to be impris-oned or exiled during the operation.[129] Although President Arbenz had been exiled, the idea of executing him had also been touted. There were other casualties of US intervention. The repressive operatives of successive military regimes

---

128 Stephen M. Streeter, "Interpreting the 1954 U.S. Intervention in Guate-mala: Realist, Revisionist, and Postrevisionist Perspectives," 61.
129 Kate Doyle and Peter Kornbluh, "CIA and Assassinations: The Guatemala 1954 Documents."

murdered more than one hundred thousand civilians, something that would not have happened had the US allowed the democratically elected leader, Arbenz, to remain in power.[130]

Even when the decisions of some US officials have ultimately led to destabilization and even war in Central America, there are still good guys in white hats among history's villains. They are the brave, moral individuals who recognized the harm their government's intervention was inflicting and they tried to stop it.

After the Nicaraguan revolution, discussed in Chapter 2, a movement against the Sandinistas sprouted: a counterrevolution, also known as the "Contras."

The US government feared that neighboring Central American countries, particularly El Salvador, would also experience a communist revolution.[131] The Contras were right-leaning and willing to fight communist or socialist groups, making them akin to US ideals. That's why, in December 1981, President Ronald Reagan signed a secret directive authorizing an expenditure of nineteen million dollars to conduct paramilitary operations in Nicaragua.[132]

However, as Contra attacks continued throughout 1982, often killing civilians along the way, some members of Congress labelled the policy as immoral and illegal. They recognized

---

130 "Ex-President Arbenz of Guatemala Dies," New York Times, January 28, 1971.

131 Ex-President Arbenz of Guatemala Dies."

132 "The Counterrevolutionaries ("The Contras")," Understanding the Iran-Contra Affair, Brown University, accessed February 15, 2020.

that this type of interventionism had negative effects, and they were ready to stop it. Consequently, congressman Edward Boland (D-MA), Chairman of the House Intelligence Committee, passed an amendment "prohibiting the use of funds 'for the purpose of' overthrowing the government of Nicaragua," coined the First Boland Amendment, on December 21, 1982.[133]

Congressman Boland certainly deserves a white hat.

History doesn't look back as fondly at others in US government. In 1986, several top US officials came up with the idea of overcharging Iran for the weapons they sold them and using the surplus to fund the Contra resupply operation and other covert activities—challenging the First Boland Amendment. The officials set up a miniature CIA to deliver arms without breaking the amendment.[134]

The consequences of this covert activity were horrific. Scrutiny over US involvement with the Contras reveals their role in a major human rights violation. A US lawyer, Reed Brody, went to Nicaragua on a fact-finding mission, collecting eyewitness statements by people affected by the contra counterrevolution and summarizing his findings in a book. This is an excerpt that explains what happened when 350 members of the Contra band, the group supported by the US, entered the town of El Anito. The testimony is by a married couple who had ten children:

133 "The Counterrevolutionaries ("The Contras")," Understanding the Iran-Contra Affair.
134 The Counterrevolutionaries ("The Contras")."

"The contras arrived at our house. We were all on the floor because they had mortars and gunfire. They stayed about an hour in the house, taking everything...They were very proud of the arms that they received from Reagan, saying that the arms that the Sandinistas had weren't good. They asked for gasoline and burned down the house, including the ENBAS warehouse [government center for the distribution of basic products] which we ran. They left us naked in the street. They also killed six people from the community."[135]

I am certain that US officials, even those who intervened in Central American countries and whose actions had deadly consequences, did not have bad intentions. They did not wear the black hat on purpose, nor did they hope to harm people's livelihoods. During the Cold War era, they probably believed that they were wearing the white hat, and that these countries were being saved from evil communism.

The lesson the US has yet to learn is that actions do, indeed, have consequences—sometimes deadly consequences—regardless of one's good intentions. Thus, history continues to repeat itself.

In a May 2017 special report entitled "US-funded police linked to illegal execution in El Salvador," *CNN* reports: "The United States has quietly funded and equipped elite paramilitary police officers in El Salvador who are accused of illegally executing gang members."[136]

---

135 Reed Brody, *Contra Terror in Nicaragua: Report of a Fact-finding Mission, September 1984-January 1985:* (Boston: South End Press, 1985).

136 Nick Paton Walsh, Barbara Arvanitidis and Bryan Avelar, "US-funded police linked to illegal executions in El Salvador," *CNN*, 2018.

Central American leaders are still the puppets, and US officials are the real protagonists or antagonists. The roles often switch. Sometimes the United States it the savior, providing the poor countries of Central America with aid. But sometimes, behind closed doors, they put on the black hat, intervening in ways that unbalance the weak region.

CONCLUSION: ILLUSION OF PROGRESS?

———

Macondo, a small town in the middle of nowhere, evolved through time. It started off as a town with only a few adobe houses that encompassed a small territory, isolated from the outside world. The town experienced civil wars and a plague that brought about death and despair. Later, it went through economic development after the construction of a train that, for the first time, connected it to the outside world, allowing an influx of modern technologies into the once secluded town.

The Buendía family lived in Macondo for a century. Through the stories of the Buendía family, the illusion of progress drags on through time, as the town grows and develops. Until we realize that, all along, the historical progression of time in Macondo was cyclical, a repetition of a series of events that stretch out from one generation to the next. Even the names of the Buendía family are repeated throughout each generation, particularly the names Arcadio and Aureliano.

Macondo is the fictional town of my favorite book, *One Hundred Years of Solitude,* by Gabriel García Márquez, that tells the story of seven generations of the Buendía family.

At the end of the book, one of the Aurelianos, a century later, opens a parchment that the first Aureliano had received from a gypsy called Melquíades, containing the hidden truth about the destiny of the Buendía family:

"It was the history of the family, written by Melquíades, down to the most trivial details, one hundred years ahead of time... Melquíades had not put events in the order of man's conventional time, but had concentrated a century of daily episodes in such a way that they coexisted in one instant."[137]

In this town and in this family, history is predetermined, all part of a cyclical mold that will inevitably go on and on and on.

The illusion of progress, characterized by access to innovation unlike any ever seen in Macondo, was but a ploy. Although the railroad connected the town to the world and allowed innovation through new technologies, it also made Macondo vulnerable. Thanks to the railroad, wealthy foreign capitalists came in and established a banana plantation, oppressing the town's citizens. Despite the illusion of progress brought about by fancy technologies like the phonograph, Macondo's people suffered the consequences.

---

137   Gabriel García Márquez, *One hundred years of solitude* (London: Penguin Books, 2014), 421.

In a book, the notion that progress is an illusion and that history is cyclical is interesting. In real life, in Central America, it is terrifying.

Circling back to where we began in this book, I dove into the civil wars and social revolutions in Central America that prompted the first waves of migration, precisely because the issues back then are the issues today: violence exists, citizens are unprotected, and life is hard for certain groups. In the previous chapter, I also brought up US interventionism, which was detrimental to the region years ago and is still detrimental today. Like in the town of Macondo, despite an illusion of progress, it seems like the episodes are so similar between decades that they are "coexisting in an instant."

As a Central American myself, the last thing I want is for history to repeat itself. This isn't a made-up tale about fictional Arcadios or Aurelianos or someone else who appeared in that book. It is about a real region with people whose lives are at stake, people who migrated in the 80s because of civil wars and other structural issues, and still migrate today for similar reasons.

I love Honduras. I love its foods and its culture. I love it with all my heart because it will always be my home. But what I love most is its amazing people. I love the people who can chat with you about their lives for hours, people who will open up to you about all the hardships they've endured, people who have dreams of growing old enough to see their children grow up to build a better future, people with no resources, sometimes living in poverty, trying to thrive in an environment that kept pushing them back. There are the people who dreamed of a better place where the grass is greener; they see another country with relative stability, like Costa Rica, as a better alternative to their lives at home. The United States, the region's main sponsor and poster child of justice and democracy, to many seemed like the place to be.

Growing up, I heard countless stories of warriors.

I have never forgotten those people, those faces. When you read about them in academic journals and reports, it can be easy to view them as statistics: X percent of the population lives in poverty, Y percent did not finish school, Z percent is unemployed, and so on. But when I found opportunities to meet them—whether on the sidewalk in Columbia Heights, the Progreso Market in Mount Pleasant, or in the back of an Uber—these "statistics" bravely ripped open old scars and shared their stories with me, simply because I cared enough to ask. And when I listened, suddenly they were no longer stats to report or data to analyze. They became real, big-hearted human beings with real stories of strife and struggle.

I created this book as a platform for migrants' stories to reach a society very much in need of hearing them. Central American migrants are not evil people. They're not coming to take our jobs. They aren't blood thirsty criminals. They are simply people who happened to be born in countries with weak states, destabilized by years of intervention. I'm baffled by the patronizing rhetoric coming from a country that has many problems of its own.

Despite my impression that the United States was a perfect country before coming here, I have become disillusioned.

Like a broken record, the United States also suffers from episodes that unveil structural issues; these play on repeat, in a loop.

I wrote this chapter during a very sad reality that still exists in the United States: police brutality against the Black community. The protests led by the Black Lives Matter movement after the killing of George Floyd, a man murdered by a police officer who knelt on his neck while other bystanders (including police officers) watch. His murder is reminiscent of how police in Central America are incapable of properly protecting the citizens they vowed to protect. It is also reminiscent of the killing of Rodney King years before, in Los Angeles. I see how the Black community and many more Americans have joined in the streets in anguish, pain, and sadness after seeing that years after the end of the country's Civil War, racism still exists.

I realize that Central America's fragmentated nations—with territories acting autonomously from the state—are almost a mirror image of the United States' polarization and fragmentation in the current political climate. My region continues to fight to improve, thinking that it is so far behind, and yet meanwhile, Central America's main sponsor, a nation many Central Americans look up to, is suffering from many similar state deficiencies: a judicial system and police system that do not protect all its citizens and that favor certain groups over others.

Perhaps the cyclical nature is not only applicable to Central America. Can it be that in the United States, the country that has molded Central America for many years, progress is also but an illusion?

I want to believe that the answer is no.

Writing this book has been a challenge; it has been difficult to hear sad stories, knowing that to some of it meant opening closed wounds. Putting these stories in the context of a broken region has upset me at times—a feeling of impotence because little progress has been achieved. And yet one of the biggest challenges was trying to provide a solution to the issue of migration. Because, in my opinion, migration is not the problem.

What truly worries me late at night is that many Central Americans don't have a decent livelihood. Essentially, the structural problems that exist in Central America lead people to decide to leave because many individuals have been unprotected from violence, have no safety net or unemployment protection, and are abandoned. I know so, because even for me—someone who had a good life in Honduras—I experienced many difficult moments in which I really doubted my parents' decision to raise me there. I saw people close to me, friends and neighbors, experience unimaginable things. Even though many of the events were normalized, the fact that more vulnerable groups are even more at risk of experiencing these realities is unsettling.

But I also love Honduras so much. And I know it has potential. I think Central Americans know that too, and they want to see change.

That is why I wrote this book: so that policy-makers and other individuals learn that, for some time, we have been living in a cyclical history and it is time to get out. The problems Central Americans face today look and sound a lot like the problems they faced in the 80s and 90s. A powerful country like the United States, one that many Central Americans look up to, cannot intervene for self-interest then turn their backs on the collateral damage of their actions when it's at their doorstep. Failing to learn from past mistakes and neglecting the issues unfolding in Central America, will only doom history to another cycle of repeated events. Unlike Aureliano, I want Central America to break free from this loop.

ACKNOWLEDGEMENT

Primero que todo, gracias a mi familia—Papiyo, Lilo, Gabo, Abuelita, Caro, Nati y Dani—por apoyarme en todas mis locuras, y compartir sus historias conmigo.

Thank you, Em, for helping me find my zen in moments of despair. You are my favorite.

Thank you to my editor, Pea, the most intelligent and insightful person ever. Without you, I could never have written a book I am proud of.

Special thanks to Eric Koester. Your energy is unlike anything I have ever encountered. Without you, I would have never had this wonderful opportunity.

Thank you to my beta readers for your insights and for supporting me from early on. Every time I saw an e-mail from one of you, it motivated me to keep going:

Adriana Sierra Leal   Izzy Mattoon

Adriana Viteri

Aeden O'Connor

Aimee Lansdale

Alberto Flores Madero

Alec Brevé Mazzoni

Alejandra Quiroz

Alejandro Rodríguez Zamora

Ali Matthews

Amanda Chatupron-Lacayo

Ana Barahona

Ana Lucrecia Murillo

Ana Rosabal

Andrea Ar Di

Andrea Rodriguez

Andrea Zúñiga

Andrew Elam

Angela Lopez

Angelo Rivero Santos

Anna Coby

Annabelle Timsit

Antonio Quintanilla

Aracelly Arguedas Wollenweber

Aubrey Wahl

Beatriz Bechelli

Bianchi Suarez

Brenda Villatoro

Carlos Carpizo

Carlos Fortin

Carlos Galeano

Carolina Quintero

Cassandra LaChase

Jasmine Rogers

Javier Ochoa

Jenil Doshi

Jonathan Ettinger

Jose Altamirano

Jose Duran

Joshua Davis

Juan Romero-Casillas

Julia Yansura

Kathya Araya

Kaya Afflerbach

Kjell Fenn

Laura Castro

Laura Gama

Lauren Allen

Leana Hernandez

Lilliana Tapia Arguedas

Luis Andres Simbaña Caiza

Luis Breve

Luis Joy Perez

Manuel Ossenbach

Marco Aurelio Odio

María del Mar Guardia

María Fernanda Pérez Argüello

Maria Garibay

Maria Teresa Agurcia

Marie Obando

Marielena Octavio

Marielena Valdés

Marielle Kafie

Mario Lopez-Garelli

Catherine Mucciolo

Chandler Payne

Chris Valdes

Christina Huntzinger

Clara M Rodriguez-Rojas

Claudia Alarco Alarco

Clayton Newton

Daniel Leonard

Daniela Forero

Danny Castro

Dante Gomez

Dayana Moncada

Devin Crane

Diana Chaves

Diana Ramirez

Diana Rojas

Elcior Santana

Elena Campos Chacón

Eleno Castro

Emerson Souza

Eric Koester

Erick Mitchell-Velásquez

Erika Moyer

Erika Skafel

Erin Bailey

Ernesto Fernández

Espartaco Gonzalez Arteaga

Fabiana Pineda

Francisco Palmieri

Gabriel Donato

Gabriel Rodríguez

Marta & Wendell Barron

Matt La Pan

Mauricio Quintero

Max Magerman

Meagan Moran

Melissa Castillo

Melissa San

Michelle Chacón

Mimi Liu

Moisés Sánchez Galindo

Monica Rodriguez

Muriel van de Bilt

Natalia Quintero

Nicole Carolin

Nicole Pochet Ballester

Nicolle Hernandez

Orlando Caceres

Paul Trapido

Pea White

Raul Maynigo

Rodolfo Scannone Chavez

Ronnie Quintero

Rosa Cuppari

Roxana Amador R

Sabrina Fantoni

Samila Inacio Dutra

Santiago Agurcia

Sara Rockefeller

Sarah Hechtman

Sarah Karas

Sartaj Singh

German A. Henry	Sawyer Thomas
Glenn Jones	Silvia Badilla Arroyo
Govind Bhutada	Sofia Chamorro
Guillermo Tapia Campos	Sofia Vargas
Hannah Odio	Sylvia Cesar
Ingrid Fiallos	Tamar Haddad
Isa Benson	Violeta Barcenas
Ivonne Rodriguez	Violeta Bermudez

Thank you to Julia Yansura, Manuel Orozco, Melissa Vida, Chris Valdes, Esther Anino, Rafael Jerez, Alejandro Kafatti, Stacey Pirtle, Ariel Ruiz, Vanessa Leandro, and Tim Gindling for sharing your insights and knowledge.

Special thanks to all those amazing women who helped me spread the word about my book: Alejandra Quiroz and Sussan Garcia from Central American Voices Podcast, Maria Garibay and Diana Contreras from Insightful Babes, and Christine Osoria, author of *Rosalia - the Honduran American.*

Most importantly, thank you to all my interviewees who shared their experiences, stories, and opinions. You were my main motivation throughout the journey.

APPENDIX

INTRODUCTION

Camarota, Steven A., and Karen Zeigler. "Central American Immigrant Population Increased Nearly 28-Fold since 1970," *Center for Immigration Studies* (Washington DC, November 2018). https://cis.org/sites/default/files/2018-11/central-america-nov-18_0.pdf

"Central American Migration: Root Causes and US Policy." Congressional *Research Service*, June 2019: 1.

del Carmen, Giselle and Liliana D. Sousa. "Human Capital Outflows: Selection into Migration from the Northern Triangle." *World Bank*, Policy Research Working Paper 883, 2018. http://documents1.worldbank.org/curated/en/653631518451652402/pdf/WPS8334.pdf

Menjívar, Cecilia, and Andrea M. Gómez Cervantes. "El Salvador: Civil War, Natural Disasters, and Gang Violence Drive Migration." *Migration Policy Institute*, August 2018. https://

www.migrationpolicy.org/article/el-salvador-civil-war-natural-disasters-and-gang-violence-drive-migration

Orozco, Manuel. "Central American Migration: Current Changes and Development Implications." *Inter-American Dialogue*, November 2018: 8. https://www.thedialogue.org/wp-content/uploads/2018/11/CA-Migration-Report-Current-Changes-and-Development-Opportunities1.pdf

"Plan of the Alliance for Prosperity in the Northern Triangle: A Road Map." *Inter-American Development Bank.* September 2014, 1-10. http://idbdocs.iadb.org/wsdocs/getdocument.aspx?docnum=39224238

"Population 2019." World Bank Data. https://databank.worldbank.org/data/download/POP.pdf

¿Qué ofrece el Plan Alianza para la Prosperidad?" *Inter-American Dialogue:* 1-2. https://www.thedialogue.org/wp-content/uploads/2016/03/AlianzaParalaProsperidad_Final_3.16.16.pdf

Rodríguez, Ana Patricia. "Becoming 'Wachintonians' Salvadorans in the Washington, D.C., Metropolitan Area." *Washington History,* Fall 2016. http://www.dchistory.org/wp-content/uploads/2020/03/02-Becoming-Wachintonians-Salvadorans-in-the-DC-Metro-Area-by-Ana-Patricia-Rodriguez-28-2-Copy.pdf

Villiers Negroponte, Diana. "The Surge in Unaccompanied Children from Central America: A Humanitarian Crisis at Our Border." *Brookings Institution,* July 2014. https://www.brookings.edu/blog/up-front/2014/07/02/the-surge-in-unac-

companied-children-from-central-america-a-humanitari-
an-crisis-at-our-border/

CHAPTER 1

Booth, John A., Christine J. Wade, and Thomas W. Walker. *Under-standing Central America: Costa Rica, Nicaragua, El Salvador, Guatemala and Honduras: from Independence to the Present.* Boulder, CO: Westview, 2005.

"El Salvador" The Center for Justice & Accountability. https://cja.org/where-we-work/el-salvador/

Menjívar, Cecilia and Andrea Gómez Cervantes. "El Salvador: Civil War, Natural Disasters, and Gang Violence Drive Migration." *Migration Policy Institute.* August 29, 2018. https://www.migrationpolicy.org/article/el-salvador-civil-war-natural-disasters-and-gang-violence-drive-migration

Roig-Franzia, Manuel. "Oscar Arias Sanchez reflects on 25 years since Central American peace accords." *The Washington Post* (August, 2012). https://www.washingtonpost.com/lifestyle/style/oscar-arias-sanchez-reflects-on-25-years-since-central-american-peace-accords/2012/08/22/e396ea92-e7d8-11e1-a3d2-2a05679928ef_story.html

"Salvador Archbishop Assassinated By Sniper While Officiating at Mass; Churchman Was Known as Outspoken Advocate of Justice and Rights Advocate of Human Rights ARCHBISHOP ROMERO SLAIN IN EL SALVADOR" *The New York Times,* March 1980. https://www.nytimes.com/1980/03/25/

archives/salvador-archbishop-assassinated-by-sniper-while-officiating-at.html

CHAPTER 2

Feingold, Spencer. "Nicaragua scraps controversial social security reforms." CNN, April 2018. https://edition.cnn.com/2018/04/22/americas/nicaragua-scraps-controversial-social-security-reforms/index.html

Guerrero, Kay and Theresa Waldrop. "Death toll in Nicaragua protests reaches 273, human rights group says." *CNN* (July 15, 2018). https://www.cnn.com/2018/07/15/americas/nicaragua-deaths-protests/index.htmlOrozco, Manuel. "Country Profile: Nicaragua." *Inter-American Dialogue,* 2018: 1. https://www.thedialogue.org/wp-content/uploads/2018/11/Nicaragua-2018-migration-profile-1.pdf

Riding, Alan. "Chronic Repression and Corruption Undermine the Somozas' Alliances." *The New York Times,* Feb 26, 1978. https://www.nytimes.com/1978/02/26/archives/a-dynasty-under-siege-in-nicaragua.html

Romero, Luis. "Since April, more than 300 people have died protesting in Nicaragua. Here's why." *Quartz,* July 2018. https://qz.com/1329198/protests-in-nicaragua-against-president-daniel-ortega-have-resulted-in-over-300-deaths-since-april/

"Somoza Family: Nicaraguan Family." *Encyclopedia Brittanica.* https://www.britannica.com/topic/Somoza-family

CHAPTER 3

Abuelafia, Emmanuel, Giselle Del Carmen, Marta Ruiz-Arranz. "Tras los pasos del migrante: Perspectivas y experiencias de la migración de El Salvador, Guatemala y Honduras en Estados Unidos." *Inter-American Development Bank* (December 2019). https://publications.iadb.org/es/tras-los-pasos-del-migrante-perspectivas-y-experiencias-de-la-migracion-de-el-salvador-guatemala-y

Carrillo, Ana Lorena. "Indias y Ladinas: Los Ásperos Caminos de las Mujeres en Guatemala," in *Antología del pensamiento crítico guatemalteco contemporáneo,* edited by Guillermo Toriello et al, 617-631.Buenos Aires: CLACSO, 2019.

Martin, Maria. "Killings of Guatemala's Indigenous Activists Raise Specter of Human Rights Crisis." All Things Considered, *NPR,* January 22, 2019. https://www.npr.org/2019/01/22/685505116/killings-of-guatemalas-indigenous-activists-raise-specter-of-human-rights-crisis

Ramos, Jerson and Acan - Efe, "Efraín Ríos Montt padece demencia vascular," *Prensa Libre,* August 18, 2015. https://www.prensalibre.com/guatemala/justicia/juicio-contra-rios-montt-continua-con-audiencia-para-determinar-su-condicion/

Schrage, Elliot J. *Promoting International Worker Rights through Private Voluntary Initiatives.*Iowa: The UI Center for Human Rights, 2004. *The University of Iowa: Center for Human Rights.* 2004. Web. 6 Apr. 2017.

The Associated Press. "Exhibit traces history of Voting Rights Act." *NBC News,* 2005.

Verité, "Research on Indicators of Forced Labor in the Supply Chain of Coffee in Guatemala" (2016). https://www.verite. org/wp-content/uploads/2016/11/Research-on-Indicators-of-Forced-Labor-in-the-Guatemala-Coffee-Sector__9.16.pdf

CHAPTER 4

Bargent, James. "Explicación de los significados ocultos de los tatuajes de las maras de Honduras." *InSightCrime,* September 3, 2014. https://es.insightcrime.org/noticias/noticias-del-dia/explicacion-significados-tatuajes-maras-honduras/

Boffey, Daniel. "As Trump closes US doors to migrants, Latin Americans look to Europe." *The Guardian,* July 10, 2019. https://www.theguardian.com/world/2019/jul/10/latin-american-migrants-europe-belgium-spain-eu

Carballo, Carlos A. "El Salvadors crime prevention policies from Mano Dura to El Salvador Seguro." *Calhoun: The NPS Institutional Archive* (2015). https://calhoun.nps.edu/bitstream/handle/10945/47916/15Dec_Carballo_Carlos.pdf?sequence=1&isAllowed=y

Charles, Jacqueline, David Smiley, Monique Madan. "Federal appeals court decision brings Trump administration closer to ending TPS." *Miami Herald,* September 14, 2020. https://www.miamiherald.com/news/nation-world/world/americas/haiti/article245727245.html

Convention and Protocol Relating to the Status of Refugees. 1951 Convention, Resolution 2198 (XXI) adopted by the United Nations

General Assembly. United Nations High Commissioner for Refugees. https://www.unhcr.org/en-us/3b66c2aa10

Cruz, José Miguel Cruz. "Central American *maras*: from youth street gangs to transnational protection rackets." *Global Crime* 11, no. 4, (2010): 379-398. https://www.tandfonline.com/doi/full/10.1080/17440572.2010.519518?scroll=top&needAccess=true

Dudley, Steven and Héctor Silva Ávalos. "MS13 in the Americas: How the World's Most Notorious Gang Defies Logic, Resists Destruction." *InSite Crime* and *Center for Latin American & Latino Studies,* February 16, 2018. https://www.justice.gov/eoir/page/file/1043576/download

"For Central Americans, Fleeing to Europe May Beat Trying to Reach US" Forschungsgesellschaft Flucht und Migration eV (2019). Accessed, May 10, 2020. https://ffm-online.org/for-central-americans-fleeing-to-europe-may-beat-trying-to-reach-u-s/

Gallón, Angélica. "La estratégica razón por la que ahora la MS-13 prohíbe a sus miembros llevar tatuajes." *Univisión Noticias,* March 18, 2018. https://www.univision.com/noticias/trending/la-estrategica-razon-por-la-que-ahora-la-ms-13-prohibe-a-sus-miembros-llevar-tatuajes.

Gammage, Sarah. "El Salvador: Despite End to Civil War, Emigration Continues." *Migration Policy Institute,* July 26, 2007. https://www.migrationpolicy.org/article/el-salvador-despite-end-civil-war-emigration-continues

Meissner, Doris, Faye Hipsman, T. Alexander Aleinikoff. "The US Asylum System in Crisis: Charting a Way Forward." *Migration Policy Institute*, 2018: 18. https://www.migrationpolicy.org/research/us-asylum-system-crisis-charting-way-forward

Menjívar, Cecilia and Andrea Gómez Cervantes. "El Salvador: Civil War, Natural Disasters, and Gang Violence Drive Migration." *Migration Policy Institute*. August 29, 2018. https://www.migrationpolicy.org/article/el-salvador-civil-war-natural-disasters-and-gang-violence-drive-migration

Ribando Seelke, Clare. "Gangs in Central America." Congressional Research Service, 2016. https://fas.org/sgp/crs/row/RL34112.pdf

Selee, Andrew, Silvia E. Giorguli-Saucedo, Claudia Masferrer, and Ariel G. Ruiz Soto. "Strategic Solutions for the United States and Mexico to Manage the Migration Crisis." *Migration Policy Institute*, (July 2019). https://www.migrationpolicy.org/news/strategic-solutions-united-states-and-mexico-manage-migration-crisis

US Law Library of Congress. The United States Department of Justice. El Salvador: Gang Violence, by Norma C. Gutiérrez, 008435. 2012. https://www.justice.gov/sites/default/files/eoir/legacy/2013/11/08/gang_violence2012.pdf

US Library of Congress. Congressional Research Service. Anti-Gang Efforts in Central America: Moving Beyond the Mano Dura? by Clare Ribando Seelke. 2007. https://fas.org/sgp/crs/row/RL34112.pdf

CHAPTER 5

Alandete, David. "Alejandro Giammattei: Admito que Guatemala es un problema de seguridad para Estados Unidos." *ABC Internacional,* September 2019. https://www.abc.es/internacional/abci-alejandro-giammattei-admito-guatemala-problema-seguridad-para-estados-unidos-201909080257_noticia.html?ref=https:%2F%2Fwww.google.com%2F

Alvarez, Priscilla. "What happened to the migrant caravans?" *CNN,* March 2019. https://www.cnn.com/2019/03/04/politics/migrant-caravans-trump-immigration/index.html

Brown, Thad A. *Migration and Politics: The Impact of Population Mobility on American Voting Behavior.* Chapel Hill, NC: The University of North Carolina Press, 2011.

Gaborit, Mauricio, Mario Zetino Duarte, Carlos Iván Orellana, and Larissa Brioso. "Chapter 4. El Salvador." Essay. In *Childhood and Migration in Central and North America*, edited by Karen Musalo, Lisa Frydman, Pablo Ceriani Cernadas.

Center for Gender and Refugee Studies, 2015. https://cgrs.uchastings.edu/sites/default/files/Childhood_Migration_Human-Rights_FullBook_English.pdf

Girod, Desha. *Explaining Post-Conflict Reconstruction.* Oxford University Press, 2015.

Jones, Jeffrey. "New High in US Say Immigration Most Important Problem," *Gallup* (June 2019) https://news.gallup.com/poll/259103/new-high-say-immigration-important-problem.aspx

Keller, Allen, Amy Joscelyne, Megan Granski, and Barry Rosenfeld. "Pre-Migration Trauma Exposure and Mental Health Functioning among Central American Migrants Arriving at the US Border." *Plos One*12, no. 1, 2017. https://doi.org/10.1371/journal. pone.0168692.

"Migrant caravan: What is it and why does it matter?" *BBC News,* November 2018. https://www.bbc.com/news/world-lat-in-america-45951782

"Support for Central Americans." Monitor on Psychology. American Psychological Association, 2019. https://www.apa.org/ monitor/2019/10/support-central-americans.

Zong, Jie and Jeanne Batalova. "Central American Immigrants in the United States in 2013." *Migration Policy Institute,* September 2015. https://www.migrationpolicy.org/article/central-american-immigrants-united-states-2013

CHAPTER 6

Pebley, Anne R. and Luis Rosero-Bixby. "Demographic Diversity and Change in the Central American Isthmus" *Rand Corporation,* 1997. https://www.rand.org/pubs/conf_proceedings/ CF135/index2.html

Sorrentino, Joseph. "Train of the Unknowns: Crossing the Border Isn't as Hard as Getting To It." *Commonweal,* November 2012. https://www.commonwealmagazine.org/ train-unknowns

CHAPTER 7

Orozco, Manuel. "Latin America and the Caribbean Migration from Weak and Failing States." *Inter-American Dialogue,* (July 2019): 5-6.

Weber, Max. Politics as a Vocation. *From Max Weber: Essays in Sociology,* (2014):89-140. doi:10.4324/9780203759240-8

Valdes, Christopher and Theodore Grisold, Olancho (2017) documentary.

CHAPTER 8

"Forced to Flee Central America's Northern Triangle: A Neglected Humanitarian Crisis." *Médecins Sans Frontières,* May 2017. https://www.msf.org/sites/msf.org/files/msf_forced-to-flee-central-americas-northern-triangle_e.pdf

Steven Dudley. "InSide: The Most Dangerous Job in the World." *InSite Crime* (March 2011) https://www.insightcrime.org/investigations/inside-the-most-dangerous-job-in-the-world/

Steven Dudley and Michael Lohmuller. "Northern Triangle is World's Extortion Hotpost" *InsightCrime.* (July 2015) https://www.insightcrime.org/news/brief/northern-triangle-world-extortion-hotspot/

CHAPTER 9

Abuelafia, Emmanuel, Giselle Del Carmen, Marta Ruiz-Arranz, "Tras los pasos del migrante: Perspectivas yexperiencias de la

migración de El Salvador, Guatemala y Honduras en Estados
Unidos." *Inter-American Development Bank,*2019. https://pub-
lications.iadb.org/es/tras-los-pasos-del-migrante-perspectiv-
as-y-experiencias-de-la-migracion-de-el-salvador-guatemala-y

"The World Bank in Nicaragua." *The World Bank,*Web, accessed
September 25, 2020. https://www.worldbank.org/en/country/
nicaragua/overview

CHAPTER 10

BBC News. "El escándalo que llevó al ejército a controlar los
medicamentos en Honduras." June 19, 2015. https://www.bbc.
com/mundo/noticias/2015/06/150619_america_latina_salud_
honduras_corrupcion_militares_amv

Carling, Jørgen, Erlend Paasche, and Melissa Siege. "Finding
Connections: The Nexus between Migration and Corruption." *Migration Policy Institute* (May 2015). https://www.
migrationpolicy.org/article/finding-connections-nexus-be-
tween-migration-and-corruption

Del Águila, José Pablo. "Conamigua tiene una pobre ejecución de
presupuesto en doce años de vida." *Prensa Libre,* September
17, 2020. https://www.prensalibre.com/guatemala/migrantes/
conamigua-tiene-una-pobre-ejecucion-de-presupuesto-en-
doce-anos-de-vida/

Melgar, Ana. "Fiscalía de Honduras investiga posible fraude en
compra de hospitales móviles para atender pacientes de covid-
19" *CNN,* June 2020.https://cnnespanol.cnn.com/2020/06/24/
alerta-fiscalia-de-honduras-investiga-posible-fraude-en-com-

pra-de-hospitales-moviles-para-atender-pacien-
tes-de-covid-19/

Morales Rodas, Sergio. "Recepción de migrantes deportados
ha costado más de Q8.4 millones." *Prensa Libre,* August
10, 2020. https://www.prensalibre.com/guatemala/migrantes/
recepcion-de-migrantes-deportados-ha-costado-mas-de-q8-
4-millones/

Mucino, Kristel. "WOLA Report on the International Commission
against Impunity in Guatemala (CICIG)." *WOLA.* June 2015. h
ttps://www.wola.org/analysis/wola-report-on-the-internation-
al-commission-against-impunity-in-guatemala-cicig/

Ruiz Soto, Ariel G., Rodrigo Dominguez-Villegas, Luis Argueta,
and Randy Capps. "Sustainable Reintegration: Strategies
to Support Migrants Returning to Mexico and Central America." *Migration Policy Institute,* January 2019: 23.

Torres, Damaris. "Honduras: escriben en puente Fe y Esperanza, ¿Dónde está el dinero, #Honduras lo exige?" *Radio
HRN,* August 2020.https://www.radiohrn.hn/honduras-es-
criben-en-puente-fe-y-esperanza-donde-esta-el-dinero-hon-
duras-lo-exige

Transparency International. "Corruption Perceptions Index."
Accessed February 15, 2020. https://www.transparency.org/
en/cpi/2019/results

Wirtz, Nic. "Corruption Network in Guatemalan Health System
Exposed." *Americas Quarterly,* May 22, 2015. https://www.

americasquarterly.org/blog/corruption-network-in-guatema-
lan-health-system-exposed/

CHAPTER 11
"A Call to Action: Los Angeles' Quest to Achieve Community
Safety." *Advancement Project*, 2013.

Morison, Patt. "Patt Morrison Asks: Connie Rice."*Los Angeles
Times*, December 28, 2011. https://www.latimes.com/opinion/
la-xpm-2011-dec-24-la-oe-morrison-connie-rice-20111224-
story.html

Orozco, Manuel. "One Step Forward for Central America: The
Plan for the Alliance for Prosperity," *The Inter-American Dialogue,* March 16, 2016. https://www.thedialogue.org/
blogs/2016/03/one-step-forward-for-central-america-the-plan-
for-the-alliance-for-prosperity/

Ramírez Irías, Lester and Rafael Jerez Moreno. "Informe sobre
la impunidad en homicidios: Periodo de estudio 2010-
2017." *Alianza por la Paz y la Justicia,* June 2019.

Rice, Connie. "Civil Rights Attorney On How She Built Trust With
Police." Interview by NPR Staff, *Code Sw!tch,* NPR, December 5, 2014. Audio, MP3, 7:03. https://www.npr.org/sections/
codeswitch/2014/12/05/368545491/civil-rights-attorney-on-
how-she-built-trust-with-police

Rice, Connie. *Power Concedes Nothing: The Unfinished Fight for
Social Justice.* New York: Scribner, 2014.

Umemoto, Karen. *The Truce: Lessons from an L.A. Gang War.* Ithaca, NY: Cornell University Press, 2018

CHAPTER 12

Abuelafia, Emmanuel, Giselle Del Carmen, Marta Ruiz-Arranz. "Tras los pasos del migrante: Perspectivas y experiencias de la migración de El Salvador, Guatemala y Honduras en Estados Unidos." *Inter-American Development Bank* (December 2019). https://publications.iadb.org/es/tras-los-pasos-del-migrante-perspectivas-y-experiencias-de-la-migracion-de-el-salvador-guatemala-y

Hall, Anthony L. "Migrant Remittances, Livelihood, and Development." In *Moving Away from Poverty,* edited by Deepa Narayan, Patti Petesch, 307-332. Washington DC: World Bank, 2007.

Lopez-Cordova, Ernesto and Alexandra Olmedo, "International Remittances and Development: Existing Evidence, Policies and Recommendations," *INTAL/ITD Occasional Paper, no.* 41 (January 2006). https://ssrn.com/abstract=888531

Newland, Kathleen and Carylanna Taylor. "Heritage Tourism and Nostalgia Trade: A Diaspora Niche in the Development Landscape." *Migration Policy Institute,* September 2010. https://www.migrationpolicy.org/research/heritage-tourism-and-nostalgia-trade-diaspora-niche-development-landscape

Orozco, Manuel and Julia Yansura, "Remittances and Financial Inclusion: Opportunities for Central America," *Inter-American Dialogue,* February 1, 2015. https://www.thedialogue.org/

analysis/remittances-and-financial-inclusion-opportuni-
ties-for-central-america/

Orozco, Manuel, Laura Porras, and Julia Yansura. "Remittances
Scorecard: 2016." *Inter-American Dialogue,* December 16, 2016.
https://www.thedialogue.org/analysis/remittance-transfers-
scorecard-2016-test/

Orozco, Manuel. "One Step Forward for Central America:
The Plan for the Alliance for Prosperity." *Inter-American
Dialogue,* March 16, 2016. https://www.thedialogue.org/
blogs/2016/03/one-step-forward-for-central-america-the-plan-
for-the-alliance-for-prosperity/

Orozco, Manuel. "Remittances to Latin America and the Caribbean: Emerging Challenges: 2019," *Inter-American Dialogue,* 2019." *Inter-American Dialogue,* 2019.

"Proyecto Oportunidades para mi Comunidad," *USAID* and
Inter-American Dialogue, July 2019. https://www.thedialogue.
org/wp-content/uploads/2019/08/OFMC-impact-presentation.
pdf

Terry, Donald F. and Steven R. Wilson. "Beyond Small Change:
Making Migrant Remittances Count." *Inter-American Development Bank,* 2005. https://publications.iadb.org/publications/
english/document/Beyond-Small-Change-Making-Migrant-
Remittances-Count.pdf

CHAPTER 13

Brody,Reed. *Contra Terror in Nicaragua: Report of a Fact-finding Mission, September 1984-January 1985.* Boston South End Press, 1985.

Doyle, Kate and Peter Kornbluh. "CIA and Assassinations: The Guatemala 1954 Documents." *National Security Archieve Electronic Briefing,*Book No. 4. https://nsarchive2.gwu.edu/NSAEBB/NSAEBB4/

"Ex-President Arbenz of Guatemala Dies." *New York Times,* January 28, 1971. https://www.nytimes.com/1971/01/28/archives/expresident-arbenz-of-guatemala-dies.html

Lakhani, Nina. "Did Hillary Clinton stand by as Honduras coup ushered in era of violence?" *The Guardian*, August 31, 2016. https://www.theguardian.com/world/2016/aug/31/hillary-clinton-honduras-violence-manuel-zelaya-berta-caceres

Nooruddin, Irfan. "Analysis for the Organization of American States (OAS)." *Organization of American States,*2017. https://www.oas.org/fpdb/press/Nooruddin-Analysis-for-OAS-Honduras-2017.pdf

Paton Walsh, Nick, Barbara Arvanitidis and Bryan Avelar, "US-funded police linked to illegal executions in El Salvador." *CNN,* 2018. https://edition.cnn.com/interactive/2018/05/world/el-salvador-police-intl/

Streeter, Stephen M. "Interpreting the 1954 US Intervention in Guatemala: Realist, Revisionist, and Postrevisionist Perspectives." *The History Teacher,* Vol. 34, No. 1 (Nov 2000), 61-74. https://www.jstor.org/stable/3054375?seq=1

CONCLUSION

García Márquez, Gabriel. *One hundred years of solitude.* London: Penguin Books, 2014.

Made in the USA
Las Vegas, NV
12 December 2020